EXPOSING THE DARK SIDE OF UFO RESEARCH!

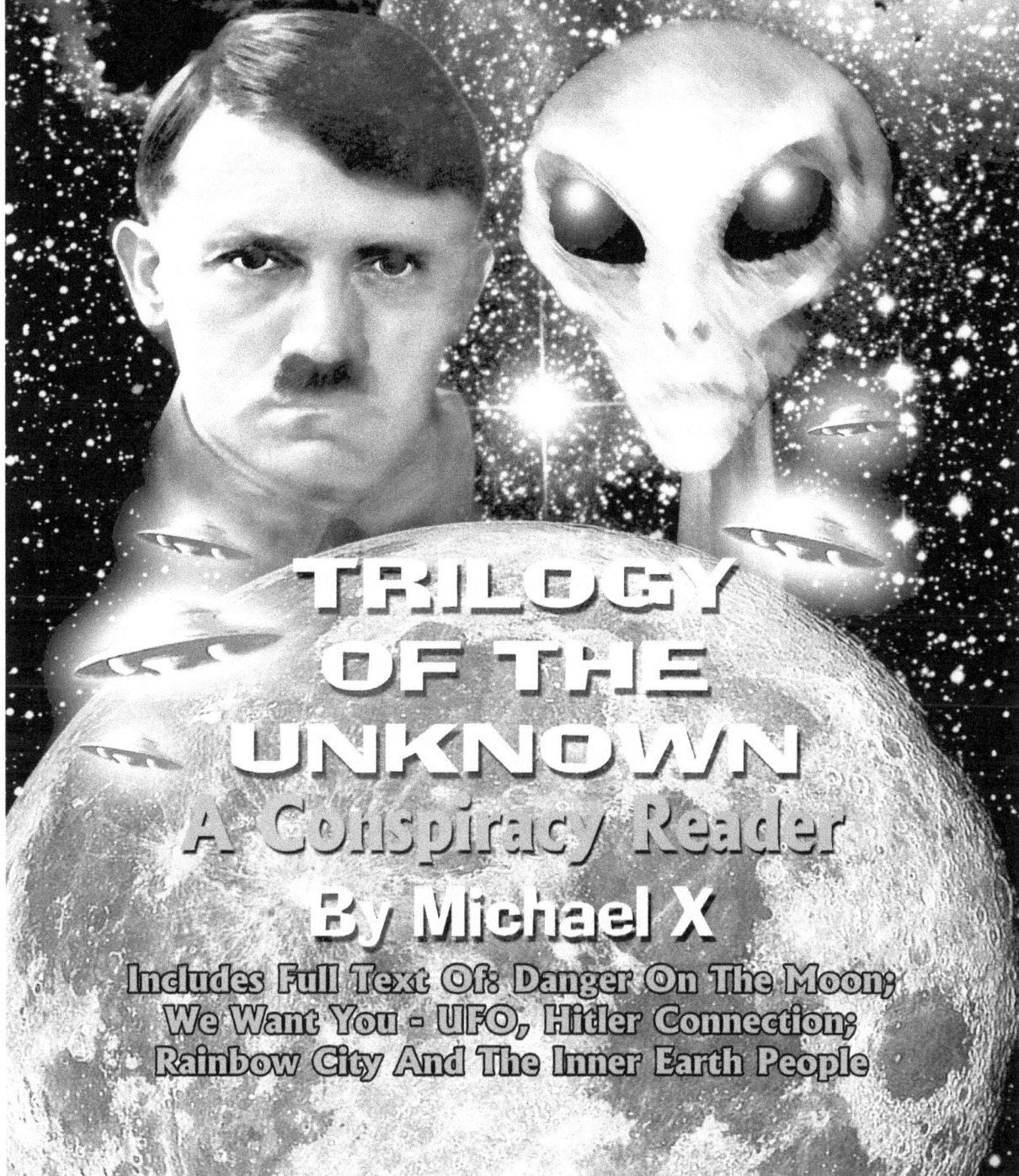

TRILOGY OF THE UNKNOWN

A Conspiracy Reader

By Michael X

Includes Full Text Of: Danger On The Moon;
We Want You - UFO, Hitler Connection;
Rainbow City And The Inner Earth People

Global Communications

Trilogy of the Unknown
By Michael X
& Timothy Green Beckley

EAN: 978-1-60611-107-9
ISBN: 1-60611-107-8

Timothy Green Beckley: Editorial Director
Carol Rodriguez: Publishers Assistant
Sean Casteel: Associate Editor
Cover Art: Tim Swartz

Printed in the United States of America
For free catalog write:
Global Communications
P.O. Box 753
New Brunswick, NJ 08903

Free Subscription to Conspiracy Journal E-Mail Newsletter
www.conspiracyjournal.com

Contents

The Mysterious Michael X The Terrifying Side of His Encounters

Michael X was one of the greatest avatars of the early UFO/New Age movement of the 1950s. He spoke with great articulation and sincerity at many of the well attended outdoor conventions held annually at Giant Rock, a private landing strip just out of Joshua Tree in the hot Mohave Desert of Southern Calif. He spoke calmly and collectively about the arrival of the silvery spaceships, dubbed flying saucers, explaining how they were piloted by friendly space beings from this solar system and way beyond.

On a mission of peace and harmony, Michael hailed the arrival of the Space Brotherhood whom he believed were materializing here to offer assistance in any way possible to elevate our consciousness to a more harmonious one . Their goal? Allowing us to join the cosmic league of nations, a federation of spiritually advanced worlds who exist all around us in this and other dimensions, whether we believe it or not!

I guess you could call Michael X a guru of sorts, though he didn't head a religious cult nor was he looking to attract a fanatical following in the manner of other more self absorbent "masters" of universal wisdom. No! Michael X was an avatar in the true sense of the word – an advocate for all of humanity. So that he didn't become part of a cult of personality, Michael refused to reveal his last name but added the X after his first name as sort of a symbol that represented all of the mysteries of our world and the space and time we inhabit, even if we had not officially acknowledge the legitimacy of others hob knobbing among the stars.

Short in stature, but a giant in his thinking, little is know or has been written about Michael X's background. We do know his last name was Burton and he was a salesman before being engulfed with the UFO contactee movement. I did speak to him once but he never would reveal anything about his past, preferring to let his "accomplishments" speak for themselves.

If one owned a complete collection of Michael X's monographs, which I estimate number around 25 and were self published by his Futura Press from roughly 1956 through the late 60s or early 70s, one might be able to put together some incomplete biographical notes.

We know that Michael Barton was residing in Los Angeles when he found his life changed when his best friend Jim became very ill with a condition that baffled the best doctors. While meditating over his buddy's deteriorating condition, Michael found he was able to receive telepathic communications beamed to him from more advanced cosmic souls.

Not wanting to alienate his business clients, but desperate to get the information he had collected out to a growing number of adherents in UFO and New Age philosophy, he began to self-publish courses and monographs under the pseudonym of Michael X. His work was read and distributed widely as believers and skeptics alike instinctively took to what he had to say and recognized the importance of its content.

You see, Michael X didn't just write about lights in the sky --or about close encounters for that matter. No, Michael X got his information first hand via telepathy from his extraterrestrial "guides." And they taught him much; everything from health secrets to how their understanding of science, philosophy and religion, could possibly propel us forward into a New Age of reason and enlightenment.

And above all else – Michael X shared what he learned from the "Venusians" -- whom he said were his closest acquaintances – in a series of very concise study guides which he sold mainly at UFO and metaphysical meetings, but also advertised in publications like *Fate* and Ray Palmer's *Flying Saucers From Outer Space* magazine. In fact, truth be told, I was selling Michael X's books when I was 15. We would advertise them in our little mimeographed publications and Michael would drop ship them to our readers. He had books on cosmic telepathy, how to initiate contact with the UFOnauts, health secrets, visions at Fatima, Nazi UFO secrets and so forth. Before he vanished from the scene he sold most of his books to Gray Barker of Saucerian Press. When Barker passed I purchased all the remaining copies and had them lying around in various cubbyholes for years but now feel it is important for these monographs to be brought back into circulation.

I do not know if Michael X is still with us or not. If he is I know he will not be resentful of the fact that we have decided to compile and reissue some of his most vital writings for an entirely new generation to consume and gain knowledge from.

We have already reprinted his work *Flying Saucer Revelations* as a bonus section in the book *Vi Venus: Starchild,* now obtainable directly through us or on Amazon.Com of course.

Insider Information

But, as it turns out, Michael X's career was not only involved with the sweetness and light aspects of the New Age movement, but had stumbled upon the darker side of UFOlogy which frightened him so much that he eventually left behind the work he loved so much. This is a little known "secret" about Michael X that I don't believe has ever been presented before.

I got this information from a buddy, Dr. Frank E. Stranges author of *Stranger at the Pentagon* and a fairly good friend of Michael's. For years they crossed paths speaking at the same venues mainly California-based metaphysical centers and Spiritualist churches, who were open to ideas involving extraterrestrials, doubtlessly because of their highly evolved secular appeal.

As you can see from reviewing the presentation of the material published in this compilation of Michael X's varied work, he did not rule out the negative aspects of what he was involved in; though I don't' believe he ever felt his life would be placed in great jeopardy as it eventually turned out to be.

In this Trilogy Of Terror we present what might be considered to be information on the seamier side of the subjects at hand.

Here is information on Nazi UFOs, which Michael spoke about years before anyone else dared touch the theory that German scientists had stumbled upon a revolutionary form of propulsion and had constructed disc-shaped devices that they had hoped would help them win the war. There is also a warning from the space people to get our tail off the moon and never return – OR ELSE! And if you think David Icke was the first to write about reptalians roaming the earth, guess again for Michael told about the existence of a race of serpents running around inside Rainbow City as part of an inner earth contingent.

Apparently, he went TOO FAR somewhere along the line in releasing this information and "they" went out of their way to get him!

Call it the Psychic Mafia if you want, whatever, it doesn't make much difference. The threat turned out to be real and VERY DEADLY.

During one of his meditations a "voice" came to Michael and gave a specific place and time to meet for a face to face encounter with his supposed alien friends. They promised to reveal some information that had not been disclosed before that would be helpful in the dissemination of his work.

Michael was sent to an out of the way place in the Mojave Desert where they could be secluded from others who might see their landed ship and "turn them in."

At first when Michael got to the desolate spot he saw nothing so he sat in his car and waited. Suddenly he saw the glint of something in the sunlight. Thinking it was their glittering craft, Barton got out of his vehicle and began to walk in the direction of where he had seen the reflection.

All of a sudden, he felt something was just not right. He heard an inner voice telling him to get out of there RIGHT AWAY or he would be in big trouble. At the point of sliding back into his automobile he looked back over his shoulder and saw the men he was going to meet, with putting down their rifle which they had been pointing in his direction. The rifle was the object that he had actually seen glittering in the sunlight.

Michael quickly realized he had every reason to be concerned – frightened might be a better term. He had

his family to think of. He had second thoughts about continuing with this work, if it was going to put his and his loved ones life in danger. And so Michael X quickly retreated

from the field. Never to be heard from again. A great loss for everyone – especially for humanity who could certainly gain from his teachings (be they from extraterrestrials or not).

I did manage to get Michael on the phone by using a contact number Dr Stranges had given me. He refused to talk about what had happened, feeling it was better to leave well enough alone. But he did confirm the basic facts of the account I have just revealed, and so we should take him at his word and leave him alone and be content with reading the work he left behind for all of us to learn from.

So here are three of the most controversial works penned byMichael X during his illustrious writing and research careers. Contemplate upon this material and decide for yourself the true nature and validity of these highly controversial claims, for the outcome of our lives may very well depend upon material such as this in the end.

Timothy Beckley, Publisher
MRUFO8@hotmail.com
www.ConspiracyJournal.Com

Mysteries on the Moon –
And A Dire Warning
To Stay Away
by
Timothy Green Beckley

Some of the first reports of unclassifiable and inconsistent activity on and around the Moon were noted, believe it or not, by astronomers. Charles Fort, the dean of researchers into the unexplainable for over fifty years, scanned from the confines of a chair in some of the world's finest libraries pages from the most obscure scientific journals, documenting dozens of cases in which astronomers reportedly observed anomalous phenomenon in connection with the lunar surface.

Still other reports were found by Fort amongst the pages of brittle news journals. Combining all the evidence, these incidents are living proof that our nearest neighbor in space may not be so dead after all.

The Moon Is Not Dead
Strange Lunar Activity

1668 November - New England - A star-like point of light seen on the Moon by colonial minister Cotton Mather.

1783 - Astronomer Sir John Herschel (discoverer of the planet Uranus) reported bright lights during an eclipse - approximate brightness magnitude +4.

1787 August 18 - Astronomer Sir John Herschel reported seeing spots glowing like "burning charcoal" on the Moon.

1821 November - Astronomer Sir John Herschel reported seeing strange lights "three times in succession."

TRILOGY OF THE UNKNOWN

1794 - Astronomer Royal, Reverend Nevil Maskelyne reported to the Royal Society "lights in the dark portion of the Moon."

1794 - A Mr. Wilkins reported to the Royal Society a dim star in the dark area of the Moon.

1843 - German astronomer Johann Schroeter recorded a six-mile wide crater which he named Linne - estimated at 1,200 feet deep - while Schroeter made detailed maps of the Moon, he noticed Crater Linne seemed to be disappearing. Today, Linne crater is only a tiny bright spot with little depth surrounded by small pits of whitish deposits.

1847 - Claims made to the British Association of "luminous points" or lights on the Moon witnessed during an eclipse.

1867 - The Astronomical Register reported that a Mr. Thomas Elger claimed he observed a light suddenly appearing on the Moon and lasting for approximately two hours before disappearing.

1869 - Royal Astronomical Society of Great Britain conducted a 3-year study of mysterious lights occurring mostly in the Mare Crisium region of the Moon - small lights seen in various arrangements, sometimes triangle and sometimes straight-line formations, moving and varying in intensity as if under intelligent control. Crater Plato was also the scene of some of the mysterious activity. After approximately 2,000 observations, the lights suddenly stopped appearing.

1869 August 7 - A Professor Swift of Mattoon, Illinois reported observing several objects in flight crossing the face of the Moon during early phases of a lunar eclipse - confirmed by French astronomers, Hines and Zentmayer.

1874 - A great number of "black objects" crossing the face of the Moon were reported by the French observer, Monsieur Lamery.

1874 April 24 – Czechoslovakia – A Professor Schafarik reported to the Astronomical Registrar – XVIII, 206 his sighting of an object that was "blinding white" slowly crossing the face of the Moon and which "remained visible afterwards."

1877 February 20 – Rash of sightings – Observatory near Paris, France observed lights in the Crater Eudoxus.

TRILOGY OF THE UNKNOWN

1877 March – Great Britain – A Mr. C. Barret witnessed a bright light in Crater Proclus that was "not a reflection from the sun."

1877 June 17 - Professor Henry Harrison spotted a light on the Moon while another astronomer reportedly saw a light in Crater Bessel.

1877 – Astronomer Dr. Klein reported a "luminous triangle" on the floor of Crater Plato that was confirmed by other observations.

1899 – Luminous object spotted moving close to the surface just above the Moon by Dr. Warren E. Day near Prescott, Arizona and G. Scott of Tonto, Arizona.

More Recent Activity

In more recent times, reports of mysterious lunar activity have continued unabated. On the web at **www.cavinessreport.com/** there is an article posted by Allan Vaviness entitled "An Historical Review of Lunar Anomalies" which covers this material extensively.

1944 August 12 - A "very bright round spot of light" in center of crater, Plato.

1950 March 30 - British Astronomer, H. P. Wilkins using a15-inch (diameter) telescope observed an oval-shaped "weird glow" in the Aristarchus-Herodotus region of the Moon.

1953 July 29 - John O'Neill, science editor for the *New York Herald Tribune*, noticed what appeared to be a 12-mile long "bridge-like structure" that had not been noticed before during countless observations of that region of the Mare Crisium area (Sea of Crisis) . O' Neil was attacked by skeptical colleagues until H.P. Wilkins, then considered number one expert on lunar topography, backed up the journalist's claims. The phenomenon was later backed up by the noted astronomer Patrick Moore. The bridge was said to be at a height of 5000 feet and perhaps as long as twenty miles. Several scientists said it was definitely artificial, and looked like an "engineering job."

1953 September 16 - Rudolph M. Lippert of the British Astronomical Association noticed a flash on the Moon followed by a light that glowed yellow-orange. A possible meteor strike?

1958 - Russian astronomer Nikolai Kozyrev reported seeing a red "cloud" on or near the central peak of Crater Alphonsus which "seemed to move and disappeared after an hour." He felt it could have been volcanic activity.

There are so many similar observations that we could devote an extensive number of pages to such intelligence. Evidently there is plenty of evidence if we look for it that there is something strange going on in the heavens, and just a "short" distance a way. The question is – are these observations proof that aliens have been active on the Moon for eons, or has a secret group – or groups – of earthlings "taken charge," and gone about their strange business "up there" just beyond our reach without telling us for reasons best known to whomever is creating these lunar "disturbances?"

Regardless, we have been warned to KEEP OUR DISTANCE – not to tally about where we are not welcome. Indeed, there is an apparent danger on the Moon and we have been summarily warned not to go back.

There is every reason to believe it is a just concern!

Danger on the Moon
by
Michael X

TRILOGY OF THE UNKNOWN
DANGER ON THE MOON

BY MICHAEL X

CONTENTS

This is an Educational and Inspirational Monograph, especially written and intended for NEW AGE Students everywhere. It contains a unique and extraordinary collection of material gathered through modern-day visions, dreams and other experiences. The following Six Chapters are provided to uplift and inform.

Statements in this Monograph are based on Scientific and Super-Sensory Findings. No claim is made as to what the information cited may do in any given case, and the Publisher assumes no obligation for opinions expressed or implied herein by the Author or by those the Author quotes.

GLOBAL COMMUNICATIONS

AUTHOR'S FOREWORD

"DANGER ON THE MOON" was written at the direct request of our Space Brothers. It is intended especially for you—the New Age individual—its purpose is to guide you on the PATH TO HIGHER CONTACTS.

Since the beginning of recorded history man has been looking up at the stars and planets around him. In those early days man probably thought he was the only living creature in the entire cosmos, and thus thought of the solar system and stars only in their relationship to the different seasons. As our race developed, undoubtedly it crossed man's mind that there might be beings, somewhere out yonder, who had developed to the point of travelling vast distances of space and could possibly visit his own world.

So, when Kenneth Arnold described seeing nine "gleaming objects" travelling at tremendous speed over Mt. Rainier, no one was greatly shocked.

However, the reasons why UFOs are visiting here are just as puzzling to many people as they were back in 1947. From past Monographs we have learned that many of these visitors bring with them a program of peace, goodwill and spiritual uplifting. They are coming here to implant in our minds spiritual thoughts which are just beginning to come to the surface in our social order—especially among the young people. They tell us that on their worlds war and crime is totally unknown—and from the evidence which has been offered we tend to accept their word for this. Certainly, any "super race" who are able to travel the vast distances in time and space required to get here, should have long ago buried their axes and picked up their plows—just as the Bible indicates

we will do some day.

In the meantime, these same beings of God's wonderful creation are concerned about *our* newly discovered methods of space travel. They are also disturbed over our continued war-like efforts on earth, and the possibility that our military leaders will not extend the battle front to other worlds. My space contacts have informed me that the Lunar Command has been warning us not to take these steps, and that they will not allow them. They have said that they will not harm any of our astronauts, but will prevent them from establishing bases on the MOON.

Several other "lower consciousness" groups, unfriendly to earth, have recently passed through the "space patrol" which guards our planet from forces against which we cannot protect ourselves. Their influence is currently being shown in many of the messages now being given to our mental and audio channels and contactees.

This then is a book about these "warnings" and messages. Our friends from other worlds are saying that if we heed these "signs" there will be peace not only for us, but for the entire solar system. They will continue to protect us from "evil" entities, but we must help ourselves by beaming total love, and peace—a God Consciousness in effect.

Should we listen or ignore? The choice is ours to make.

Spiritually Yours,

MICHAEL X
Prophet of the New Age

(2)

LUNAR WARNINGS

In June, 1969, noted UFOlogist and phychic researcher, Timothy Green Beckley, stood in front of 800 speechless UFO buffs in the Charleston, West Virginia Civic Center, and predicted that if we successfully landed on the Moon there would be strange repercussions on Earth.

He predicted, at the time, that these repercussions would be serious, and would include earthquakes, explosions, fires and power failures—all as a direct result of our landing upon the lunar surface.

Beckley explained that these predictions had come from several sources, including a number, of what he termed "silent contactees," who were sending him these strange forecasts. They explained that the space people were concerned about our swift move into outer space, and the possibility, "a strong one," that we might be tempted to use the Moon for military purposes.

These amazing predictions have been coming true. Since the Apollo 11 landing on the lunar surface there has been a considerable increase in many natural holocasts. In particular, Beckley noted in an interview in the August 31, 1969, issue of the *New York Sunday News*, that Hurricane Camille had ravaged several states, causing a considerable amount of damage in property and loss of lives.

Also, on the day before the Apollo 11 shot, an entire missile complex in southern California was hit by a mysterious blackout which prevented the firing of two rockets which were to go into a polar orbit.

At almost the same time, on the other side of the world, mysterious power failures were being reported from several large cities. In fact for several years, Unidentified Flying Objects have been blamed for mysterious and unexplained blackouts. The situation is so critical that Dr. James McDonald told a Congressional hearing he believed flying saucers were behind these occurrences:

"UFOs have often been seen hovering near power facilities. There are a small number, but still too many to seem pure fortuitous chance of system outages, coincident with the UFO sighting. One of the cases was Tamora, Illinois. Another was a case in Shelbyville, Kentucky. Even the famous one, the New York blackout, involved UFO sightings. . .I interviewed a woman in Seacliff, New York who saw a disk hovering and going up and down then shooting away just after the power failure."

Recently I received a letter from a woman in Utah who has been undergoing a series of mental contacts with space beings for some years. In the past she has sent in several predictions which have been amazingly accurate in pin-pointing disasters. In this letter she told me that something strange had been happening to her lately. Instead of the peaceful contacts she had been making, in the last few months a hostile entity had been coming in with terrible threats and warnings which she knew her "friends" would never be responsible for. This is what she wrote me in part:

Dear Michael:

I am so shook up I don't know who to turn to. Since you have been a spiritual leader for many years I thought I should write to you and tell you

(3)

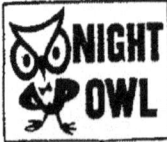

TRILOGY OF THE UNKNOWN

NIGHT OWL

SUNDAY ☼ NEWS

NEW YORK'S PICTURE NEWSPAPER ®

Vol. 49. No. 18   Copr. 1969 News Syndicate Co. Inc.   New York, N.Y. 10017, Sunday, August 31, 1969★

Saucer Expert: 'They're There'

By ALEX MICHELINI

Now that man has stepped foot on the moon and found no signs of life, can we safely write off all those tales about flying saucers as pure bunk?

"Not so fast," says Timothy Green Beckley of New Brunswick. He's one of the nation's leading authorities on Unidentified Flying Objects (UFO) and he insists it's too early to discount the existence of life on the moon.

"I don't really know how we could expect to find any signs of life when such a small portion of the surface of the moon was explored," says Beckley. "In fact, there is ample evidence to indicate that the lunar surface is being used as a base by alien beings."

Threats From Saucer Pilots

Beckley, who has received honorary certificates of appreciation from Harvard and the Asia Foundation of New York for his work in the science field, says several persons who claim to have met with saucer pilots have warned that if earthlings attempt to colonize the moon there will be serious repercussions on earth.

"These will include earthquakes, explosions, fires and power failures," he explained.

Beckley noted that in recent weeks Japan was hit by an earthquake and part of the U.S. was ravaged by Hurricane Camille. "So, perhaps some of these warnings are already coming about," he added.

If there are alien beings on the moon, what are they doing there?

Against Military Uses

"I have been informed that those who already have bases on the moon are primarily concerned in preventing us from using the moon for military purposes," he says. "The space people, I am told, want to show us they mean business. They are going to quarantine the earth until we learn to control our use of nuclear weapons."

Strange, unexplained signals from some U.S. satellites remain a mystery, the UFO expert pointed out.

"In fact, our most recent Mariner probe to Mars started sending back unscheduled transmissions which have not been explained," he says.

And what about those reports of UFO sightings by some of our own astronauts? Beckley asked.

Cites Glenn Report

He referred to comments by Col. John Glenn after his 1962 flight in which he said he was convinced "certain reports of flying saucers are legitimate." Glenn, according to Beckley, felt "the possibility of life in outer space most certainly is a possibility" and that reports of UFOs could not be ruled out.

Thus, the moon landing doesn't disprove a thing, Beckley maintains.

"We take for granted now our own explorations into outer space," he says. "So, who's to say that someone from some other planet isn't hundreds, perhaps thousands, of years ahead of us and are now looking over earth?"

Anybody got any more questions?

J 10 ● SUNDAY NEWS, AUGUST 31, 1969

TIMOTHY BECKLEY

A shot taken right off the TV as "Mr. UFO" appears as a guest on ABC's "You" program hosted by Ellie Dylan. The show was aired a few days before Halloween and involved the publisher of UFO REVIEW in investigating a haunted house on New York's busy 86th Street.

(4)

what has been happening.

Since the early 1950's, I have been in mental communication with Ashtar and several other friendly astral space beings who have told me some remarkable things. They have always been sincere, and since the Bible says, "By your fruits shall you know them", I have been inclined to accept their word for everything. Now I'm not so sure I have been doing the right thing.

Last week I had a group of associates over to the house for an inner-circle meeting. We lowered the lights as usual, and I went into a semi-trance. Always in the past I have been able to remain in complete control of my body while in this state. This time I was frightened that I would not be able to get "back in".

As soon as I was in trance, a being who called himself "Agar" came through and told me that he had a most important message that should be taken down and delivered to our scientists as well as to the government leaders of the world.

He told me that if I did not do what he requested I would be "punished" and all my friends would soon turn against me.

His warning was so negative that I hesitate to send it to you, but I know you will handle this material well and will know how to go about publishing it if you think "Agar" meant what he said.

My Blessings Brother Michael,
V.H., California

What were these terrible threats? The entity "Agar" had told "V.H." that unless the United States government allowed his group of "space people" use of their nuclear power plants for an undisclosed purpose they would cause much harm to "those in power." Obviously this type of contact does not sound like the type we have talked about in the past.

In a recent communication from the Ashtar Command, Ashtar disclosed the fact that a number of ship loads of negative beings from a distant solar system had managed to get through the space patrol which protects the Earth from all alien visitors. From what we have been able to find out, Agar is one of the leaders of this group.

One of the unique things about the Agar group is that they are able to make themselves invisible to our earthly eyes and thus can disguise themselves as ghosts and for the most part go undetected.

There have been several episodes already in which this astral traveler "Agar" has been involved. For the most part these events would seem like hoaxes to the average researcher had we no inkling of what these "invisible" beings were really up to.

In issue number 70 of *Saucer News*, James W. Moseley related in the editorial his encounter with "Agar". This encounter involved several phone calls from someone calling herself Jane Jenkings from Farmingdale, Long Island. Miss Jenkings told Jim Moseley that she was in touch with an entity named "Agar" who knew the most carefully guarded secrets about his personal life. The woman made a rendezvous with the noted saucer researcher, but failed to show up.

A few days after this a letter arrived, post marked from Long Island, inviting Mr. Moseley to meet a "spaceman" near Greystone Park in New Jersey. "The location of the proposed saucer contact turned out to be an ideal one," Jim related in Saucer News, "as it involved an area where an isolated artificial lake, high tension power lines, and a winding country road come together in one and only one spot. We took the time and trouble to arrive at the location at the appointed time; but as in the Jane Jenkings case, no one else showed up."

As Jim Moseley points out, this can hardly be considered a run-of-the-mill hoax in the light of other strange events which are taking place throughout the United States. These events include weird phone calls and visits from a group which researchers have nick-named the Men in Black—MIB. Their purpose, although unknown, is quite obviously harmful in nature. The Ashtar Command warned us some five years ago through channel Louise Hebb of Los Angeles that these things would happen as key individuals struggled to get the truth across. Only those involved in "Light" work or expanded consciousness have been bothered as the "negative" group is making a last ditch effort to drag us back down to the position we have held for centuries.

The Children of Light are under attack from all sides—negative space beings—evil astral entities—and powerful figures in all governments who are playing into their hands. The cry of the people for "peace" goes unheard as our leaders send us down the dark path of destruction.

(5)

THEY'RE ON THE MOON WATCHING US!

The German-American rocket scientist, Willy Ley, was a Flying Saucer skeptic, yet interestingly enough he died of a heart attack on the 22nd anniversary of Flying Saucers, June 24, 1969. A year earlier Ley had made this prediction: "Sooner or later, American astronauts are going to run into astronauts from another planet outside our solar system." Too bad Mr. Ley didn't stick around for another month, or at least long enough to read the censored transmission from Apollo 11 Command Service Module "Columbia," after Armstrong and Aldrin had safely lifted "Eagle" off the moon's surface and rendezvoused with Collins at 70 miles altitude. Ham radio operators on earth, tuned in to the Command Module's radio wavelength heard conversation which was not released by NASA to the radio and TV networks for re-broadcast. We quote now from an article by Sam Pepper which appeared in the September 29, 1969, issue of the weekly *National Bulletin*:

"What was it, what the hell was it? That's all I want to know."

"These (garbled) babies were huge. Sir, they were enormous."

"No, no, that's just field distortion. Oh, God, you wouldn't believe it."

"What. . .what. . .what the hell's going on? Whatsa matter with you guys. . ."

"They're there, under the surface."

"What's there? (Garbled) malfunction. . .ion. Control calling Apollo 11."

"Roger, we're here, all three of us, but we've found some visitors. . .Yeah, they've been here for quite a while judging by the installations."

"Mission Control. Repeat last message."

"I'm telling you there are other space craft out there! They are lined up in ranks on the far side of the crater edge."

"Repeat. Repeat."

"Let's get that orbit scanned and head home."

"In 624 to the fifth auto relays set. My hands are shaking so bad I can't. . .

"Film? Hell yes, the damned cameras were clicking away from up here. Did you fellows get anything?"

"Had no film left by the time (garbled) three shots of the Saucers, or whatever they were, may have fogged the film."

"Mission Control, this is Mission Control, are you under way? Repeat, are you under way? What's this uproar about UFOs? Over."

"They're set up down there. They're on the moon, watching us."

"The mirrors, the mirrors. You set them up, didn't you?"

"Yes, the mirrors are all in place. But whatever built those spacecraft will probably come over and pull 'em all out by the roots tomorrow."

(Reprinted from Borderland Sciences Research Foundation, P.O. Box 548, Vista, California 92083). End of Transcript.

Is there any evidence to verify Sam Pepper's article and the censored Astronaut dialogue? Yes, we have heard from two differend sources that ham radio operators heard the conversation. We have a recent letter from John J. Locko, Director of the World Wide Research Bureau, Lorain, Ohio:

(6)

"The article by Sam Pepper I have, also the color photo of the two flying saucers in the upper left hand corner of the photo of Aldrin staking the solar curtain. (This photo appears on page 24 of Life Magazine for August 8, 1969) In Life's "Memorial Edition" of the Apollo 11 trip, the UFOs are cropped out of the Aldrin picture taken by Armstrong. Also, a ham radio operator that lives one block from me tipped me off on the Astronaut's conversation."

Did Armstrong and Aldrin see physical UFOs and installations on and under the surface of the moon? Or were these etheric constructions, beyond the sensitivity range of normal eyesight, of TV cameras, and of the film in the motion picture and still cameras? If they were non-physical by our standard frames of reference, then the two moon pioneers are lucky to have the Aldrin photo to back up their story. This puts them in the same category as thousands of other earthians who have seen flying saucers and have little or nothing to prove it except their own word. Why should the astronauts see non-physical realities on the moon? Because their psychic sensitivity had been increased by three days of weightlessness and other sensory deprivations of deep space—but try to explain that to an academic flathead to whom such "visions" are merely hallucinations—so the controversary over "reality" will rage on we

suppose until all the material-minded Pisceans are gone from the earth. Meanwhile we UFO believers can be thankful for the Christmas present of these few shreds of evidence from the Apollo 11 landing, July 20, 1969.

APOLLODDITIES
"Noises like a fire engine surged through the airways from Apollo 11 on July 22 and left Mission Control wondering what they were. 'You sure you don't have anybody else in there with you?' Mission Control asked. There was no reply. Then came more air shattering noises again like a fire siren and sometimes like a combination of that and a buzz saw. . .No explanation was offered by Mission Control or the astronauts." Quoted from Gene Duplantier and his "Saucers, Space & Science" magazine, November, 1969.

THE UFOs, MIB, CIA AND U.S.A.F.
ALL HAVE THE SAME POLICY
"I am glad to learn that you like the literature on worldwide cooperation and brotherhood which I have sent to you. Yes, it is encouraging to know that men and women of good will the world over are communicating with each other and spreading the words of love and understanding which will eventually bring peace to troubled mankind.
"No, I have not written any papers in English on the Men in Black. A main reason is that apart from

(7)

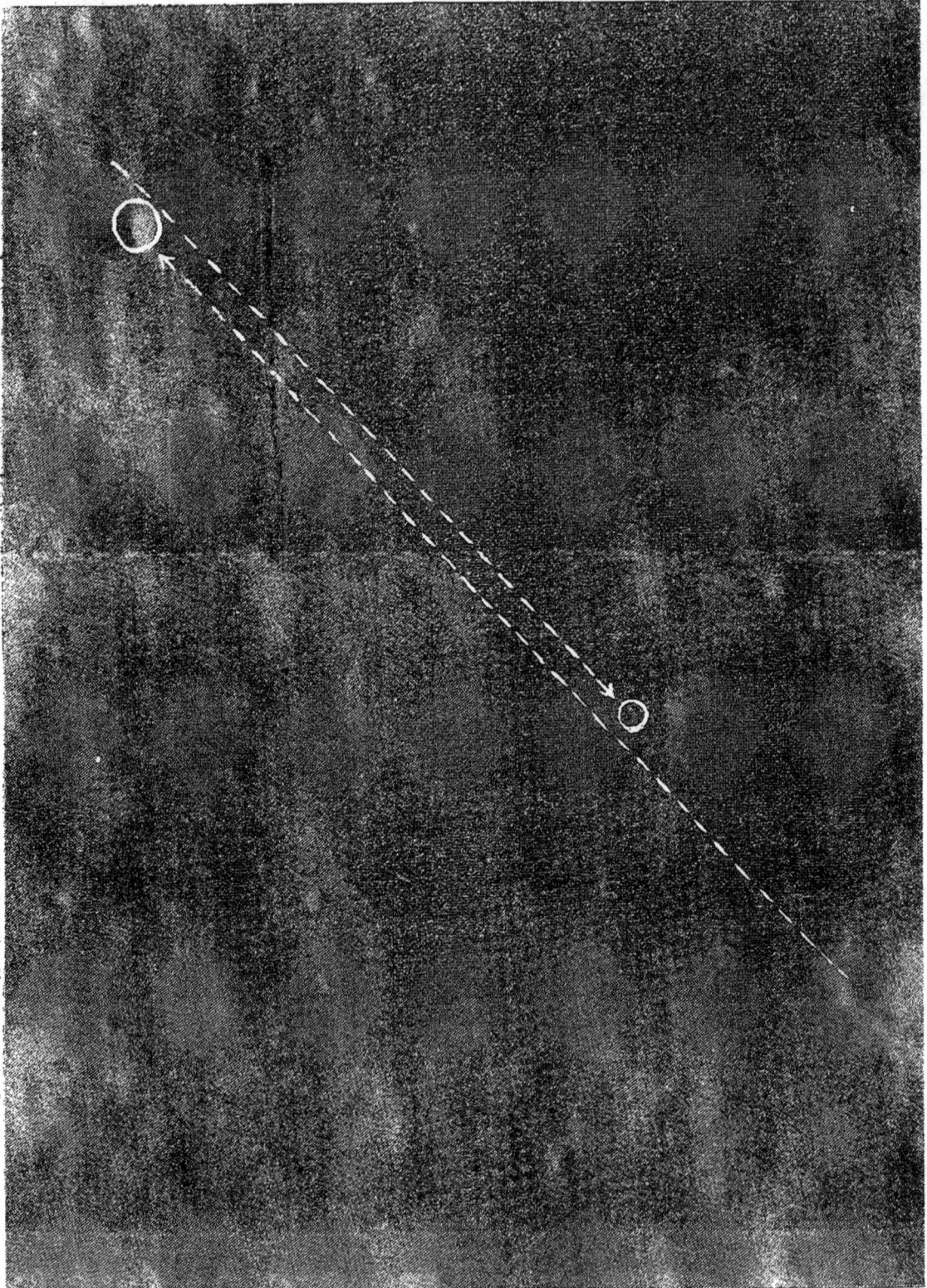

Photo of two objects inside crater Sabine D. Large object estimated to be 30 feet in diameter and of considerable weight since it has left a deep impression. Tracks indicate objects have been "rolled" in opposite direction proving they must have been intelligently moved.

a few cases the MIB are not known to appear outside America. The Men in Black appear especially in the U.S.A. and sometimes also in other North and South American countries. I find that important to observe.

"The Men in Black want the UFO contacts to be kept secret. They try to remove any evidence such as films and scare the witnesses not to talk about their experiences.

"Your CIA and your Air Force want the UFO contacts to be kept secret. They try to remove any evidence such as films and scare the witnesses so they won't talk about their experiences.

"The UFOs want the UFO contacts to be kept secret. They are careful in not leaving any evidence. They select people alone in deserted places, blackout their consciousness for about half an hour. During this time they are doing something to the human body and brain. When people wake up, they are often not aware that their consciousness has been blacked out. Soon they experience strange sensations along the spine and in the neck, but they are usually too afraid to talk about it.

"It is remarkable that the UFOs, the Men in Black, the CIA and your Air Force all have the same policy. Probably the MIB are the UFOnauts themselves or are controlled by them. One might wonder whether the CIA agents and the Air Force men aren't also controlled by the UFOs?

"If they continue their present policy, the UFOs will be able to pick up people one by one for treatment, without the rest of the population knowing anything at all about what is going on. So one day they could have treated the whole population. The science and technology of the UFOs is very advanced and we do not know what they are doing to us. As we do not know their purpose, it is potentially a very dangerous situation."

Hans Lauritzen
Copenhagen,
Denmark
(End of Article from BSRA)

WHAT OUR ASTRONAUTS HAVE SAID AND SEEN

The truth is that all of our spacemen have seen these marvelous visions of interplanetary craft—at least according to Dr. Garry Henderson who is a top man in the development of our rocket components with General Dynamics. Uncle Sam is keeping a tight lid on this information, but one of our astronauts told Dr. Henderson the facts in an off-the-record conversation.

Although a great deal of this material has been censored, some of it is still available to newsmen and researchers who know how to go about

NASA MANNED SPACECRAFT CENTER OFFICIAL PHOTOGRAPH

This photograph, made from 16mm movie film exposed by Astronaut James McDivitt, shows the unknown he observed on the 20th revolution of his four-day space flight.

McDivitt was over Hawaii when he sighted the object. He said the Gemini-4 spacecraft was turning and the sun coming across the window when he filmed the object.

McDivitt was using 16mm Eastman color film operating at six frames per second.

(9)

approaching NASA for details on these weird encounters. Their files in Washington D.C., are bulging with documented incidents which would make any UFO skeptic reconsider his position.

Here are some of those reports:

APOLLO 12—Astronauts, Pete Conrad, Dick Gordon and Allen Bean reported at least two encounters with bogeys on this historic voyage to the surface of the moon. Their first sighting was at 2:18 p.m. CST, when they radioed mission control in Houston that they were being tailed by two objects which appeared to be tumbling ahead, as well as behind their ship. The UFOs followed the Apollo 12 for a period of 18 hours before leaving at a rather rapid speed.

On November 24 (1969) with only ten minutes to splash down time in the Pacific, the space traveling trio told startled ground personnel that a bright red object had appeared directly underneath them and was flashing very brightly. It soon disappeared. No explanation was ever given.

APOLLO 8—We have from top sources that spacemen Anders, Borman and Lovell had an encounter with UFOs during the second orbit of the Moon. The sighting was of a disc shaped object which approached the capsule and flew along side of it.

During the time of the incident, ground control lost radio contact with the rocket.

GEMINI 10—The astronauts reported that they were being followed by two bright objects. John Young and Gordon Cooper told NASA's Mission Control that the UFOs seemed to be in their flight path. They vanished into space after a few seconds.

GEMINI 7—Several large and smaller "particles" seemed to be floating along with astronauts Lovell and Borman.

GEMINI 4—Major James McDivitt and Edward White were launched into orbit from Cape Kennedy on June 3, 1965. During their flight our spacemen made three different sightings of "unknowns". The first was on the 20th orbit of the space craft over Hawaii. Five frames of motion picture film were taken. They showed the object to be a large UFO with a weird contrail behind it. Another time, McDivitt told ground control that

GEMINI NEWS CENTER
Release No. 17
June 4, 1965

HOUSTON, TEXAS -- Analysis by Norad Spadat computational facilities reveals the following earth satellites were within 1000 km (about 600 miles) of GT-4 Spacecraft at the time Astronaut James McDivitt reported the satellite sighting:

Object Identification	Spadats Number	Time (CST)	Distance in Kilometers from GT-4
*Fragment	975	2:56	439
*Tank	932	3:01	740
*Fragment	514	3:04	427
Omicron Transit 4A	646	3:06	905
Omicron Transit 4A	477	3:07	979
*Fragment	726	3:09	625
*Fragment	874	3:13	905
Omicron Transit 4A	124	3:13	722
10x20 Foot Debris of Pegasus -- Shroud (A or B) not a working part of Satellite	1385	3:16	757
Yo-Yo De-Spin Weight- 2' to 3'	167	3:18	684

Pegasus B at 3:06 (CST) was about 2000 km in the proper direction to be observed by the astronauts.

*4' to 6' in length down to 15" in length, 2' to 6" in width.

NASA admits in this press release that the nearest object to McDivitt during the Gemini 4 flight was 600 miles from the space ship. This would have made it impossible to have sighted any other man made object. His three UFO sightings are thus still unidentified.

(10)

he had seen an object with long arms sticking out of it. On a third occasion the spacemen saw a bright object over China which they could not identify.

Gordon Cooper, after his 22 orbital flight of May 15 & 16, 1963 said: "I also had the idea there might be some interesting forms of life out in space for us to discover and get acquainted with. I don't believe in fairy tales, but as far as I'm concerned there have been far too many unexplained examples of unidentified objects sighted around this earth for us to rule out the possibility that some form of life exists out beyond our own world. I certainly don't pretend that the examples we know about necessarily prove anything. But,

the fact that many experienced pilots have reported strange sightings which cannot easily be explained, did heighten my curiosity about space." (Quote from book, "We Seven")

Col. John Glen, who became the first man from the U.S. to go into orbit on February 20, 1962 has since stated: "I am convinced that certain reports of flying saucers are legitimate. The possibility of life in outer space most certainly is good and thus reports of mysterious UFOs cannot be ruled out."

UFOlogists have long suspected that the UFOnauts are using the Moon as a base. The sightings of unknown craft by our astronauts near the Lunar surface would seem to verify this long held belief.

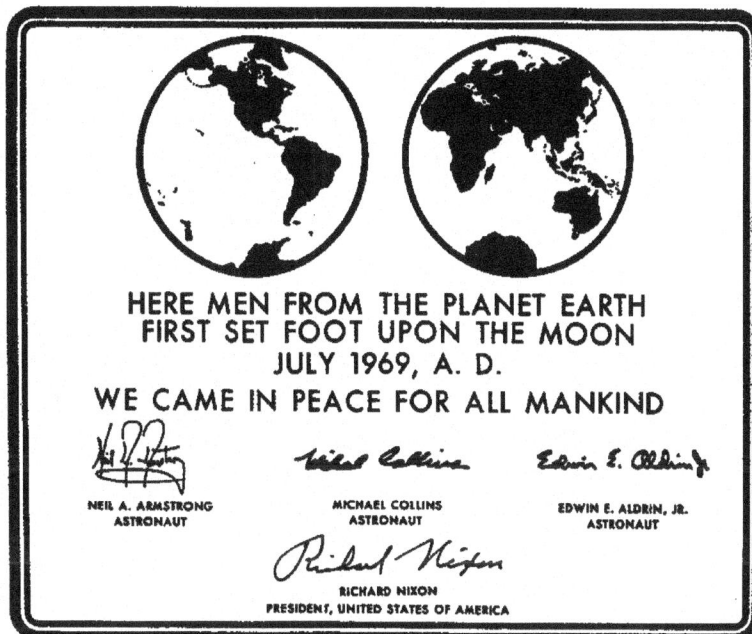

Plaque left on the Moon, July 20, 1969

(11)

APOLLO 13

On April 14, 1970, the three man crew of the Apollo 13 became involved in a nearly fatal accident on their way toward a Lunar landing.

At approximately 8:00 P.M. the next day, when the astronauts were half way from the Moon to the Earth on their premature return voyage, a space being who identified himself as Leonidas of "Moon Watch 387" came through a channel in Portland, Oregon. The channel used to relay this important information was Zelrun Karsleigh, head of the Universariun Foundation.

Leonidas has requested that this information be given as wide publicity as possible. Therefore, we are reproducing it here in full so that thousands of New Age Light seekers may be aware of this direct solar communication.

I am Leonidas of Moon Watch 387. I have desired of your Mentor to give you tonight a complete report on the Apollo 13 mission up to this point in its flight. But before I give you this, there are certain important facts which I must give you in order that you may understand thoroughly some of the concealed facts or incidents which have transpired during the flight of Apollo 13.

First of all, I will speak in the first person and if I speak of MY planet, you will understand that my base of operations is in the Spacecraft Center established quite a long time ago in the Gassendi Crater of the Moon. Therefore I will speak of my "home" Planet. I am stationed there however, temporarily, which may or may not be for a long duration depending on future conditions prevailing.

Let me inform you, my beloved friends, that there are approximately 100,000 habitants on the Moon. They are mostly, we should say 90% dwelling under the surface and in its center, for it is also hollow as is your earth. It will not be necessary for me to go into many of the ramifications, which you may do if you so desire, as to the validity of the fact that there is a Spacecraft Base on the Moon for even as few as 15 years ago, three of your astronomers in widely separated places, notably Palomar, England and Germany observed strange lights climbing up both sides of the Gassendi and Aristarchus Craters. This is a matter of record if you wish to investigate it. I just threw this in as this has been grossly overlooked by those who have administered the so-called Space Program of your earth.

Also, before I give you any report, there are certain other points of information which I desire to give you. Part of this will be a review of that which has already been given in regard to the Spacecraft which have accompanied, or rather convoyed each flight preceding this one. Now, our Spacecraft are of innumerable design and function. We have Craft which are designed specifically as what you might term "debris sweepers". As you have received a recent message or a duplication of a recent message, from beloved ORA-MON in regard to the Cosmic roadways and the debris which is littered therein in space, it may interest you to know that there is much of this and we call it Cosmic dust. It may vary from a very small particle the size of an egg floating in space to the size of an ordinary house. This is perhaps a little mysterious because of the fact that in this particular area where this occurs there is no gravity and they are

(12)

simply floating as pieces of wood or material would float upon a lake or the ocean. It has nowhere to go and is simply there and as a matter of fact to confirm what beloved ORA-MON has given you, space is full of debris.

Now you have been told by your Mentors that on the first mission there was a convoy of two of our Spacecraft, and this is correct. Perhaps he did not know the exact function of these craft. It was not *simply* for observation or to be of assistance in case of trouble, but the two Craft upon the first mission were specially designed debris sweepers. It is very difficult for me to give you this complete report without going into much, much detail which would be too long and involved. But let me inform you that the special sweepers have a function or mechanism which enable them with potential impact with any debris in space to immediately either dissolve it if it is a small particle or accelerate it out of the path of our Craft. Even at the speeds at which we travel, this is easily accomplished by methods which are foreign to your finite minds and of which I will not go into. Therefore, if it were not for the fact that our Craft convoyed your two previous flights to a successful conclusion both going and coming, they would have encountered much debris and the missions would have ended in disaster. To the second one we assigned four Craft for the pathway which they took was not exactly the same trajectory as the first, although close. There was much more debris which might have interfered with the flight.

The Apollo 13 also traversed a slightly different trajectory which was even more dangerous than the first or second and *six* of our Craft were assigned to this convoy. Now, my friends, as I repeat for you the rest of my narrative, I hope you will realize its importance and that you will, with all the facilities at your command, bring this message to the attention of those who are and were responsible for the failure and near disaster of Apollo 13.

When it was determined by our command that a "warhead" was to be fired into our planet, the six Craft which were convoying Apollo 13 were immediately withdrawn by command and 21 other specially equipped Craft were called into the area to intercept the warhead which it was contemplated to fire into our planet. This left the Apollo 13 entirely upon its own and very soon thereafter there was encountered a large piece of debris, which *your* space command classified as a meteorite. But this was not of that caliber. It was a large piece of debris which hit the module and rendered it impotent.

Now, as soon as it was determined that the missile would not be fired because of this accident, we immediately redeployed our Craft to accompany the earth craft on its remaining

trajectory and these Craft will remain with it and will do all within our power which is not limited or unlimited, to return or assist in the return of your astronauts back to the earth plane. If it becomes necessary we will assist in the minor trajectory corrections and will also endeavor to reduce the speed of the module as it enters the atmosphere of the earth as present conditions indicate that it would reach a very dangerous temperature before the final landing. All of this is contingent upon the complete cooperation of those within the capsule and the space command on the ground. Some of them know of this situation, let us say, superficially, but we wish to assure you that if there is any additional disaster, it will be because we are not able to make the necessary cooperative corrections which are necessary to bring these brave men back to earth life.

There is much more that I could tell you about your own space program which has not been revealed to the public as yet, but this is my message for this evening. However, I will conclude with the observation that those responsible for the (I will insist upon using the word WARLIKE) approach to an otherwise scientific and peaceful mission, would have been completely successful, had not their minds been bent upon this inherent tendency of your entire government in the direction of *war*. They are not contented to make war upon their earth brothers, but are also intent upon making war upon those peaceful and intelligent planets. (I still classify my Moon as a Planet).

So, if you can, with your facilities, bring this message to the attention of those authorities in charge of this project, we will greatly appreciate your efforts. I would add one more fact to that which I have given you, which is not completely within my category or authority. There is also a tendency toward lunacy in the actions of, not only your space program but the Atomic Commission as well. I will inform you that the recent atomic tests in the flats of Nevada *triggered* the disastrous earthquake in Turkey, and I will also inform you that *if the proposed explosion in the Aleutians is permitted to take place, it will widen and trigger the already unstable San Andres fault and will affect the entire Pacific Coast including your beloved city of Portland.* Therefore it is your great privilege and perogative at this time to inform both of these departments of government of their infamous and abortive efforts toward the peace and tranquillity, not only of your world, but of space as well.

(Leonidas answers some questions) *Q. When the last two flights to the Moon took place I was quite thrilled and felt that it was a good thing, but when this last one began I had a very flat feeling and a*

(13)

foreboding. *Was I accurate in this and for a reason?*
A. Not only were you correct, but thousands of sensitives all over the world sensed the same thing. You were all correct in that there *might* be a disaster taking place on this flight. Naturally it was because of the abortive effort of NASA to, in their language, try to obtain scientific information in regard to the construction of the Moon. GOOD LORD! We can give them all the information they need in regard to every section and particle of the Moon. All they have to do is ask our CHANNELS who are scattered all over the world.

Q. How would we prove this to NASA and the Atomic Energy Commission? What would back us up and what protection would be given us from reprisals from our own people?
A. My friend, I AM glad you asked that question. The only thing that we require or that you can do is to send a transcript of this message to those in charge of the space program, especially the control station at Houston, Texas. Get a copy, if possible to the 3 astronauts when they return. There is *no* proof that you can give them. In certain quarters this will be discounted and in other quarters much significance will be attached to it. I will also suggest that you send a copy to the President of the U.S. even tho it may not reach his desk.

Q. Is there a possibility that other Channels who are tuned in are getting this same message we got tonight?
A. Not only the possibility, but there are at least a dozen of them who are getting the message, not from me but from their own Mentors who will confirm much of that which I have given you, and you will be able to read it when it is published by these others. There will be a bombardment of the authorities with these telepathic messages and this will add to the authenticity and prestige of that which I have given you tonight. But WE, (WE, all of us) must use all of the facilities at hand to see that this sort of diabolical thinking on the part of several of your departments of government is brought to an end. I AM continually commuting between the Moon and the earth and watching carefully with the Craft under my command the conditions which obtain. I failed to tell you that all of these 21 Craft which were called in are standing by just above the earth's atmosphere to take part in any rescue mission which may be necessary. We hope it will not be necessary for us to take any specific hand in this but if it does become necessary, we will not hesitate to do this, altho we have told you many times that we do not interfere with any of the situations which are initiated upon the earth itself, only those which affect space and travel therein.

Q. Up to the present time our astronauts have never been permitted to express to the public the help they have received while in space. I was hoping this would be one phase in which we were permitted to know the truth. Will this be possible?
A. Your hopes will be fulfilled to a certain extent. Very shortly the secrecy which has surrounded all of this will explode like a toy balloon. That is as far as I can give you.

There are many points which I missed. The slight projectory correction which is necessary is widening somewhat and as I informed you before, if the so-called burn which will correct it is not 100% effective we will give the necessary assistance from our "degaussing" system. This is a phrase which we have coined from your nomenclature. Our ships are equipped with what you would term a degaussing system. Some of you know what this means. This generates a magnetic field or rather a complex electromagnetic field which can divert or correct any particle whether it be metal or otherwise from its directed course. We will not interfere in any way with your mechanical gadgets which to us are very crude. Yet if we feel that there is danger of disaster, then we will take a hand. Up to this point, let me inform you, my beloved friends, that it looks very good despite the news in your news media, but have no fear, for they will be returned safely to your earth. We do not wish to joke about this matter, but it is probable that the only ill effects which will accrue from the adventure will be a somewhat uncomfortable sweat bath for the astronauts which can be corrected easily with a good shower.

With that I will leave you and return you to your Beloved Mentor. I wish to thank him and you for permitting me, after a long absence for this opportunity. I have been very, very busy and there was not the occasion when I could contact you.

It was determined that this should be the Channel and Organization thru which the entire story should be broadcast to the world. So, if you will use your good services to bring this about we will be very grateful. Over and out, LEONIDAS.

Addenda to above message received Thursday morning 6 A.M. April 16.

This is Leonidas. I wish to add a paragraph to the message I gave to our Channel last night.

When it was discovered that NASA had already initiated the war-like attack upon our planet, a hasty and emergency decision of the COUNCIL was to permit the "war-head" to impinge upon our planet, rather than completely deflect it to miss the planet. However, it was deflected slightly so that the impact would be in an unpopulated area, and our 21 Craft given this assignment cushioned the impact to about one tenth of the anticipated uninhibited impact.

(14)

This hasty decision was made in order that we might have a thoroughly documented case against earthman to be used in subsequent Planetary, Solar or Galactic Councils. Another reason for the permission of the impact was that it would have been very convenient for NASA to have announced that something went awry with the shot and it missed the target, knowing nor admitting nothing of any extra-terrestrial deflection.

The above information in no way contradicts or abrogates that which I gave you last night, but at the moment of transmission (approximately 8 P.M.) all attention was focused on redeploying the convoy to give whatever assistance might be needed to get your astronauts safely back to earth. Some more difficulty will arise later this evening, but we will give whatever assistance is needed to correct it.

The Planetary and Solar Council wish to thank you for your speedy and energetic efforts in getting my message to the PEOPLE.

Over and out for now. LEONIDAS.

(15)

THE STAR LIGHT MESSENGER

Hundreds of groups now exist throughout the world which are proclaiming the heralding of a New Age! They are acting as messengers, or channels, for space beings and astral entities who are beaming messages of peace and joy to our planet. They are telling these "channels" that our world is in a critical stage, that if we don't "watch our step" we will be destroyed.

One of these channels is Jackie White Star who for more than ten years has acted as a "go between" for the space people and the people of planet Earth. His messages, unlike the type described in our previous chapter, reflect the beautiful and peaceful thoughts of advanced beings from other spheres of existence—on both physical, spiritual and astral planes.

On Easter Sunday, Jackie White Star received this telepathic message addressed to all Earth inhabitants, by "Christopher," "official spokesman for the Interplanetary Moon Council and for the King of the Moon." (Please note that since this material is transcribed without the benefit of proper editing we have made certain minor changes:)

AN IMPORTANT EASTER MESSAGE
FROM THE LUNA MOON
GREETINGS AND SALUTATIONS TO ALL EARTH INHABITANTS! This is an official, direct communication from the Divine Hierarchal Cosmic Interplanetary Council of the LUNA MOON Seat of Government. This is an official spokesman representative speaking this spring afternoon to all the beloved Earth Brothers and Sisters who have long waited to hear an official message from the inhabitants of the LUNA MOON. My name is

CHRISTOPHER, aide to the Hierarchal King of the Moon, and assistant to the Cosmic Council of our Luna Seat of Government. I am not a stranger to this channel.

This message is being transmitted as a result of an important decision of this Cosmic Solar Council.

We wish to extend our Easter greetings and Lunar blessings unto all who would be interested in the messages which are directed through the New Age publications emanating from various enlightenment groups. Earth is at a critical time in its karmic evolution, with dramatic changes facing you now, culminating in extraordinary world events.

As has been prophesied by many channels of light, at this precise time Divine orders have been ordained for the inhabitants. New changes are augmenting themselves through action of a new influx of infra-red energies into the force-field around earth. They are penetrating into the atmosphere of the Earth plane and the under-surface of the ground floor itself. These high potency energies shall change certain properties that are fundamental in your atom structure.

When the body currents encase themselves around the physical embodiment of Man they are energized by these force fields of atomic particles that comprise the very air you breathe. The habitat you dwell on is directly affected; also affected are the body functionary processes of the human man. This is considered to be the ultimate and supreme form of nature's evolutionary processes. This is only true insofar as men of earth have not been privileged to explore the sister planets and galactic sun systems throughout the Cosmic Universe.

There seems to be one pertinent, dominant

question on the lips of the students of these enlightenment groups: If life or intelligence does exist on the Moon why don't they speak to you? The seeming silence from this higher sphere is mysterious and incomprehensible to most people.

This has been a subject for much deliberation by our esteemed "council of twelve" ruling body. I admit it had been more than disconcerting in its overall meaning to most of you. It would be impossible at this time to give you a detailed analysis of the Council's reasons for the continued silence. The official specified time element has now spent itself and the specified period for new Divine Action has officiated itself into being.

This statement has been given unto me, Christopher, to proclaim to the earth.

The antiquated, outdated time element has now resolved into a new glorious Ascension of the Divine Light of the Omnipotent, Eternal God, the Great I AM, the life spark of Mankind. Man is now officially cut loose, freed from his prison of shackles and those circumstances that held him anchored to Karmic ties of centuries of the past. The hour glass for your planet has fulfilled its Karmic cycle and now the umbilical cord of past indiscretions are resolved. You might also think of your beloved planet as becoming matured. Old enough now to join her elder brothers' planetary system in new duties for the evolvement of the universe. You are a free people, with dignity, intelligence and wisdom.

This new Cosmic dispensation of higher Interplanetary law can now be given to help our young sister progress in a faster evolution upward in economic, political and world supervision. This means direct help from your Planetary neighbors in the heavens above you. Until now this has meant we could not directly meddle in your affairs or send legal ambassadors. But, now the time of new representation for the Solar Governments will be allowed to work in the open and offer their services to the various organizations and groups which will accept them.

THE SPACE PEOPLE HAVE A DIVINE PLAN FOR THE UNITED STATES

It has also been worked out in detail how a world program shall be developed to introduce to the general public our aims and future motivations to bring world self-government to fruition.

The immediate news events across your world reflect violent changes within the system of government and in the conscious thinking of men and women themselves. There must first be a strong desire in a human being to want a definite change in something he desires. It is distressing to us, your elder brothers, to see the chaotic, spasmotic, negative conditions permeating the earth at this most significant time. Be patient with these crises arising in the four corners of your globe. The backward countries are indeed affected by fluctuating influences between violent passions of the lower-self and the altruistic good of all Mankind. There will not in the coming Summer months seem to be enough wisdom in counseling these small countries to resolve conditions.

INDIA & CHINA

India and Communist China must be given more material help and intelligent enlightenment in how to bring their economies up to higher standards of living.

THE UNITED NATIONS

The U.N. shall be called for help time and time again in the coming years. They will be asked to mediate and negotiate new peace terms. There are not enough experienced men to contribute their creative talents and energies to this vast, prodigious program that Earth is experiencing at this climactic time in history.

AMERICA

Your own beloved United States shall not fare too well in their techniques to cope with the endless worsening race riots which precipitate themselves into the news.

In summation, you must discern from your own vast experience of living that in order to enact a change in life, something drastic usually augments itself into your personal world. Without negative experiences expressing in personal affairs of man the new glorious Light of all we have dreamed about could not come into being. This is the only disciplinary action that the mortal mind of man understands.

THIS IS THE TIME OF ACTION

The time of action is not way off into the distant future, as previously thought. But, only by your loving understanding and adherence to the Higher Principles of the Master's inculcation of Higher Wisdom have you now won out over darkness and atomic destruction by war instruments in your precious earth.

You will see the self-evidence of these long prophesied events come into fruition. The world will not annihilate itself, but at times will come close to it. Have no fear, for we are watching with the fatherly protection of the Father-Mother being.

Peace and Eternal Blessings pour forth abundantly from all who serve the high office in the bright, galactic golden sun of the great eternal

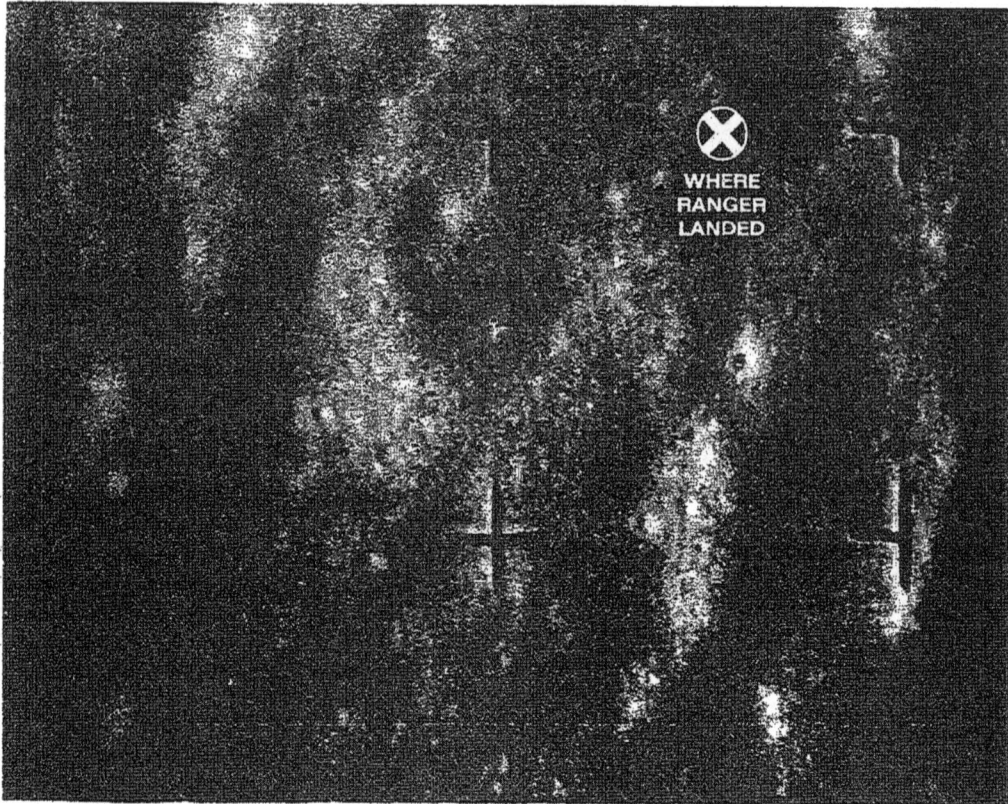

WHERE RANGER LANDED

CITIES ON THE MOON!

One of 4,000 pictures taken by Ranger VII in July, 1964 of moon. Round figures in crater at top left called rocks by authorities, presently arguing over their interpretation of the pictures. We say they are round domed hangars for flying saucers and even temporary living quarters for the Visitors . . . as a landing base from outer space before flying into our atmosphere. There was one other picture . . . further to the south east on the moon that showed "rocks", also . . . out of hundreds of craters. (Information from Laura Mundo)

Fatherhead Omnipotent.

We are your Planetary Brothers of the most High Councilship of the LUNA MOON.

End of Special Message From the Moon

What Christopher of the Lunar Council has told us in effect is being repeated by dozens of channels the world over. Even poet and folk singer Bob Dylan has told us in his music that "The Times They Are A-Changin".

The younger generation, although misguided in their use of drugs and attitudes toward sex, have done much to usher in this great New Age. Instead of being critical of their programs, we of the New Age should direct and channel their thoughts to where it will do the most good. Let us show them that the spiritual way is by far more enjoyable than the physical; that in order to experience "freedom of the mind" they do not need drugs.

After we have solved our own problems here on earth we will be ready for the biggest conquest of all—TRAVEL TO OTHER PLANETS and FACE-TO-FACE MEETINGS WITH INHABITED WORLDS!

(18)

WHAT THE SPACE PEOPLE WANT

"The SI's are here to help us, if we will only listen", says Ted Owens, an amazing psychic-contactee whose predictions have been 75% accurate.

Owens had his first encounter with "flying saucers" in Fort Worth, Texas, in the early 1960's. At the time, he was doing work with a group of "three super E.S.P. people who were quite advanced in clairvoyance and telepathy." Owens systematically used hypnotism with them, endeavoring to send their minds to seek out UFOs and establish mental communication.

This he did with considerable success. What happened next was even more amazing:

"At the time I lived with my tiny daughter, Lornie, age 8. One particular evening I was out driving along a lonely road in the Texas countryside, with my daughter in the seat next to me just after dark. Suddenly she said 'Daddy, look, what is that?' and pointed out my driver's window to the left of our car. I took one look, and immediately pulled over to the side of the road and parked. There coming across a field toward us, about 500 feet away, was a cigar-shaped object, with vivid colors streaming from it. White, blue, red and green are the colors I remember strongly now. It seemed to be floating or gliding toward us, making no noise whatsoever. It came fairly close to our car—I would say to within 50 feet—then dipped downward and vanished completely."

ONLY THE BEGINNING

After this evening, strange things began to happen! "Ideas began to come to me in a flood," Owens relates. "First these ideas helped me to write a book about healing. Then, as the years passed, something seemed to give me intelligence about national and international events, all of which later came to pass."

At first "the Philadelphia Prophet" thought that the source of this intelligence was nature itself. But after several more messages it was positively proven, "at least to my satisfaction" that a certain group of space people or interdimensional creatures to be more exact, were responsible for the things going on within his brain.

Within a few months of his amazing encounter on the Texas desert, Owens took his family to Washington where he arranged several meetings with government agencies in order to tell them what he had discovered. But they seemed unimpressed with this information. "Then one evening the intelligence came to me stronger than ever. It told me to give a man I knew in the C.I.A. a message that it would do something at the North or South Pole which would change the electro-magnetic field there, and would make the newspapers. They said that when this happened it would be absolute proof of my contact with these then unknown intelligences. Weeks passed and nothing happened. Five months passed...there it was. The South Pole UFO that parked over the two scientific expeditions, altering the electromagnetic equipment at the bases involved." This was of course widely published by the news media since it came at a peak in UFO interest.

Owens claims he gets his information through symbols. "First a triangle and rectangle popped into my mind, then the letters A, B and C," he says, making reference to an early contact.

(19)

During his early period of "training" by the SI's, they told him that they planned to use him as their "go between" with the people of Earth. What they did went much farther than the "contactee" stage. They told him that they would give him a power that would prove their existence to everyone. This power would be in the range of "PK"—the ability to control and move objects without coming into direct contact with them.

As an example of this unusual, but proven power, Owens gives the following example: "In Philadelphia the SI's told me to write to the papers and say that I would make it storm. I did so, naming the dates, and they turned loose some fine storms (this during the height of the drought). The papers wrote this up, and I was asked to appear on an important radio program in the City of Brotherly Love. The night before I was to go on radio 'they' contacted me and directed me to a typewriter, and had me type out a message from them to the American People. They told me to take it to the radio station, and they would see that the message got out. I typed it, next day went to the station and read it to a half million listeners."

Since then Ted Owens has continued to amaze many people, including radio commentators, scientists and assuredly the U.S. government—as he has continued to send copies of his "predictions" to them.

Says Owens, "The SI's would tell me to write to my contacts that an earthquake would hit California in a few days or weeks—sure enough, California had several big ones. They would tell me they would make an early hurricane off Florida, to tell my contacts—and surely enough, Hurricane Alma appeared, the earliest on record to hit the United States. They told me to warn the Government the communists were preparing to attack our ships off Viet Nam. Just two days later, they struck with a sneak torpedo boat attack. But I had called the C.I.A. and passed the message on so when the Reds struck, the U.S. was waiting for them. . .and knocked them out of the water. Always I have written to the government, scientists and friends before the various happenings, so there would be a concrete record of it all." And it has come to pass in case after case, leaving us with the only possible conclusion—that Mr. Owen's contacts mean what they say!

WHAT THE SI'S WANT

What is it that the SI's want? "They are trying to put the world into balance by cancelling out wars, hate, killing, upset weather conditions, drought, famine, etc. THEY CAN DO ALL THESE THINGS EASILY! . .But, first they want a base to work from, and they chose the United States. The hitch is they will not allow themselves or their apparatus to fall into the hands of humans, who are already destroying each other fast enough. They do not trust government officials, scientists, or military men. Unfortunately, since these are about the only three categories that are listened to, or who have any 'standing'."

Thus the SI's have a problem on their hands. They want to meet with the top leaders, including Nixon, but there is only one safe way to do this. They must use Ted Owens as a go between—a middle man.

"This is the plan they sent me with to the Government.

"The U.S. would send me to Europe with one Special Forces man, who would be a bodyguard and witness. I would be guided by the SI's to select an old deserted castle in an isolated location. I would live there for one year. Sometime during that time the Saucer Intelligence would appear to me for a face to face meeting and arrange a way to meet with the President. They would give me materials as proof. And the Special Forces man would be with me as a witness."

Why the year? "It would be difficult for agents of the United States (or some other power) to keep a trap set for one year and attempt to snare a craft."

The SI's warn that time is growing short. That only they can stop our inexorable approach to a nuclear war with the resulting deaths of countless humans and the certainty of the United States being destroyed forever. "According to them we probably have only a year or two at maximum to avoid this. No time for years of 'UFO Investigation' by teams of scientists who can only get there after the UFOs are gone and perhaps discover, if they are lucky, that there really was a UFO there."

Mr. Owen's warning has been given. . .will we accept it?

MESSAGE TO THE AMERICAN PEOPLE. . .
FROM THE FLYING SAUCER INTELLIGENCE
Sent through Ted H. Owens

We are very happy that we are able to reach the ears of human beings after trying for long long spaces of time. This human who is talking for us, we have been teaching for years in your time, and now he knows much. . .and will know much more. He can do much. You must listen to him carefully, and protect him, for if you lose him you lose your link with us, and it is not known for how long it may be until we find another human who can receive our thoughts, and send intelligence back. It would be as if you were trying to teach your earth animals how to talk, and suddenly you found one who could actually converse with you. . .and through this one animal you had an opportunity to discover the secrets of the animal kingdom.

Through us you have the opportunity to discover the secrets of the animal kingdom. Through us you have the opportunity to discover the secrets of space, of far away places, of advanced technology, but better still you have the opportunity of surviving, for as a race you are utterly doomed now, as you are flying (this is their exact words). Many civilizations before you have so doomed themselves, and destroyed themselves, and we were helpless to give them assistance and advice and powerful aid. Now for the first time in long space ages we are able, through a human's senses, to come to the aid of a good civilization and help it to survive. But we can only do so if you listen and pay attention.

We are causing, severe drought, with our machines in your skies, so that we can teach you a basic lesson. This is that our intelligence is far superior to that of earth intelligence. We can control earth people because we can control what you call weather. When, and not before, our earth human has been accepted by your government, and put to good use, then and only then will we release the drought conditions, and let rainfall come in abundance down onto your thirsty earth. We will also add pestilence and sickness and what you call accidents; we will follow the structure of events which we used in the day of the human you know as Moses, as he strove against the ruler of the great country called Egypt. As we helped Moses in that day, so shall we help the human friend we know now as Ted Owens, you call the "Rain Maker". If it pleases him to think that. . .of course we make the rain for him, but what is the difference? So that you people of the earth will believe this message we send to you, and we do not expect you to believe it unless we show proof. . .listen carefully.

From now on, in time ahead, we will lift the drought for a little, and let it rain where it is needed. Then, lest you think that it is a perchance, we will drop the curtain once more with our machines, and let the rays of the sun penetrate the bowels of the earth and dry up your rivers, your lakes, your plants, until you accept our human as our representative.

After you accept him, we have much work for him to do, for we do not speak your language, nor do we know too much, as we should, about your inner workings. It is through this human that we can learn; and it is through us that you can learn. Even now, we send the meaning of our thoughts to him, and his brain translates through pictures and feelings into your English. It is good!

Beware lest you take too long to accept our human-friend, for then we must strike a hard blow at your country which spurns him. . .to punish your country as you would punish a child which persists in misbehaving. After your country has accepted our link and we are able to proceed to keeping earth humans from the time old habit of erasing themselves as civilizations, we will make your earth a wonderful place, the way it should be. We have no wish to rule you, or dictate to you. . .we only wish, as friends, to know you, and teach you, and let you be happy. We are not of flesh and blood such as you. Our composition is that of your grasshopper, so that our bodies will compress and expand with spacework. We have no blood, but different chemicals inside ourselves. We are small, but have the ability to reverse our body electricity at will, and this gives us strength to move and to carry great burdens; makes us very strong. Language difficulty makes it difficult for us to send a stream of highly advanced technical information through our human-friend's mind for translation, since he is not a scientist, and must therefore translate as he understands. But for a beginning it is good.

And may we ask you please be careful not to pursue our crafts in your curiosity. . .not to attack us with your weapons, simply because we are not like yourselves. When our human friend is in an area, please do not have planes overhead, because you do not know it but we will have our craft there as well. . .we have methods that make our ship so that your earth eyes cannot see them, at times. You ask if there is anything else, earth friend. Just that, we are happy, and excited for you, and your people, and for us. Be patient and be careful, for we cannot risk losing our human friend-link. THAT IS ALL. . . .

(21)

HOW TO CONTACT "POSITIVE" SPACE PEOPLE

In order to make the "highest" possible contact with our space brothers you must have a whole-hearted desire. As I stated in my earlier book, "The Secrets of Higher Contacts", this must include meditation and thought of a deep-souled intensity.

You must also believe that they exist just as you do; that they can respond to you.

Above all you have to be honest with yourself. You must ask yourself, "Why Must I Contact Space Beings?" Selfishness and one's personal problems or "hang-ups" rule out many potential channels. Purity of motive and sincerity are the attitudes which will leave you open for the messages which you seek most.

Remember that there are many different types of Space People: (1) Physical beings whose vibratory frequency is considerably higher than ours, (2) Etheric beings who dwell in the etheric regions around the earth and around other planets, (3) Celestial beings involved in the cause side of creation (Angelic Beings). The first two classifications are made up of our Elder Brothers and Sisters who have already advanced to the next "Hier Arc" of Soul, mind and body progress. They make use of Spaceships, Space Stations and mental contact methods.

NINE GUIDE LINES
OF THE ASHTAR COMMAND
FOR HIGHER COMMUNICATIONS

The Ashtar Command lists nine guide lines for attempting contacts with "positive" entities and space beings. We suggest that these guide lines be adhered to as closely as possible:

1. *Do not try to contact the Space People.*
   A. They can contact you at any time or place they choose to in any form that they wish to use, depending on their evolvement. Attempting to contact them through "drugs" or "deep trance" methods leaves you open to negative forces who are not usually who they pretend to be.
2. *Prepare yourself spiritually for some useful work.*
   A. This does not mean religious practices of an orthodox nature. This means a conscious effort in attuning to that which is the highest, most beautiful, and ethernal within one's self.
   B. By work we mean anything that will in some manner help those around you to find upliftment, peace and inner joy.
3. *Live each day in service to the Creator.*
   A. By their works the Space People know them, and are able to judge by your aura if you are truly worthy of being part of their work upon earth.
   B. Your aura not only tells your past but is a good and reliable way to tell what you are best able to accomplish spiritually.

(Author's Note): If you live each day in service to the Creator you cannot possibly attract "negative" forces who feed only on the ego of undeveloped souls. If you are positive you can only attract positive. If you are negative you will attract negative. It can be no other way.

4. *Live each day as if it were your last.*
   A. Collect your mental baggage so that all which is of lasting nature can be moved at

(22)

once, all else left behind. Live so at any time or place you can turn your back upon the past without regret or backward glance.

   B. Gather unto yourself all your dreams and desires of service to God and man, for these are your wealth.

5. *Negative breeds fear and doubt.*

   A. Evil loves the unprepared, the confused and the ignorant.

   B. Spiritual understanding is the KEY to all UFO activity, both negative and positive. Spiritual guidance is offered to all who seek it sincerely and open-heartedly.

6. *The Earth is a battleground.*

   A. Remember in all that you do that the forces of evil employ ships of great size and beauty just as do the good forces.

   B. Unprepared Earthlings who seek contact must not do so without knowledge of how to set up a positive force field and hold it around themselves.

(Author's Note:) The easiest way to do this is to envision a white shield around your body. This will protect your spirit and physical body from any outside entity which may seek to take command of your mind during space contacts.

7. *Establish a contact with your God-Head* (or "Secret X" as previously identified in my teachings).

   A. No power on Earth nor from any realm outside the earth can harm one who dwells in perfect accord with his own Higher Self.

   B. This contact is waiting any and all who choose to place it in the area of the most important thing in their life.

(Author's Note): To contact your God-Head or "Secret X" it is essential to bring more tranquillity, more balance and more self-control into all thoughts, feelings and actions. As stated in Chapter Three of "Secrets of Higher Contact," here is how to do this. As you go about your daily activities, no matter where you may be or what you might be doing, think of your "Secret X". Think of it as a perfect blend of Light, Love and Life. Or if you prefer, as Intelligence, Harmony and Power. A balanced trinity. Think of it with joy. When your trinity of Power, Harmony and Intelligence are blended in your consciousness so that they become one unit, that is when you may reach your Higher Self. Then it is that you may hear the voice of your own immortal spirit whispering within your soul.

8. *Meditation and concentration bring awareness.*

   A. Be worthy of contact by the Etheric Forces by being apart from the flesh pursuits of the world. To be *in* the world but not *of* the world should be your goal.

   B. Meditate upon perfection—upon that which you would change from evil to good, from sickness to health, and from ignorance to understanding.

   C. Concentrate on being a balanced human; for you can be of no real service in an unbalanced condition, to the Space People or to yourself.

(Author's Note): My own contacts have repeated to me several times that it is okay to lecture and write on these subjects, but this should be only second to the main purpose. You are no good to the Space Brothers unless you are good to yourself. You must be able to function in a rational manner and deal with people in everyday situations. Because, if we are to tell other people about the Golden New Age, we must also show them that our way of life is as "normal" as theirs—only more advanced. The writing and the lecturing should be left up to those skilled in such matters, as to teach improperly will do more harm than good.

9. *The Kingdom of God is built by Light, Truth and Understanding of Spirit.*

   A. Radiate light, think light and you shall attract that which you seek to be, a creature of Light.

   B. Seek Truth, demand Truth and it shall be given to you. This is a Universal Law, and to know and use this understanding is wisdom.

   C. You are spirit no matter what form you are in now, and to know yourself and to be true to that inner knowledge is the greatest of all keys—for it brings the Kingdom of Heaven within you and enables you to express the Sonship of God.

In the next few years, ten thousand of us are to be contacted. If you are to be one of those "selected" for the "Great Plan" you must live by Universal Laws, not by old beliefs and traditions. You must make a clean start. Do it today by expressing your inner most "Cosmic" feelings. Release your "Secret X" or Inner-Self and make it a part of your life. Think as one of the greatest inspired works of all time tells you—Do unto others as you would have them do unto you. Let all your hates, fears and emotions evaporate into the ether.

After you have cleaned up your "spirit being," you will not only be ready for positive space contacts, but you will have opened up an entirely new higher-self. Astral Travel, Clairvoyance, PK Powers, Visions, will all come naturally. Some of the best prophets and psychics of today are also contactees and channels.

(23)

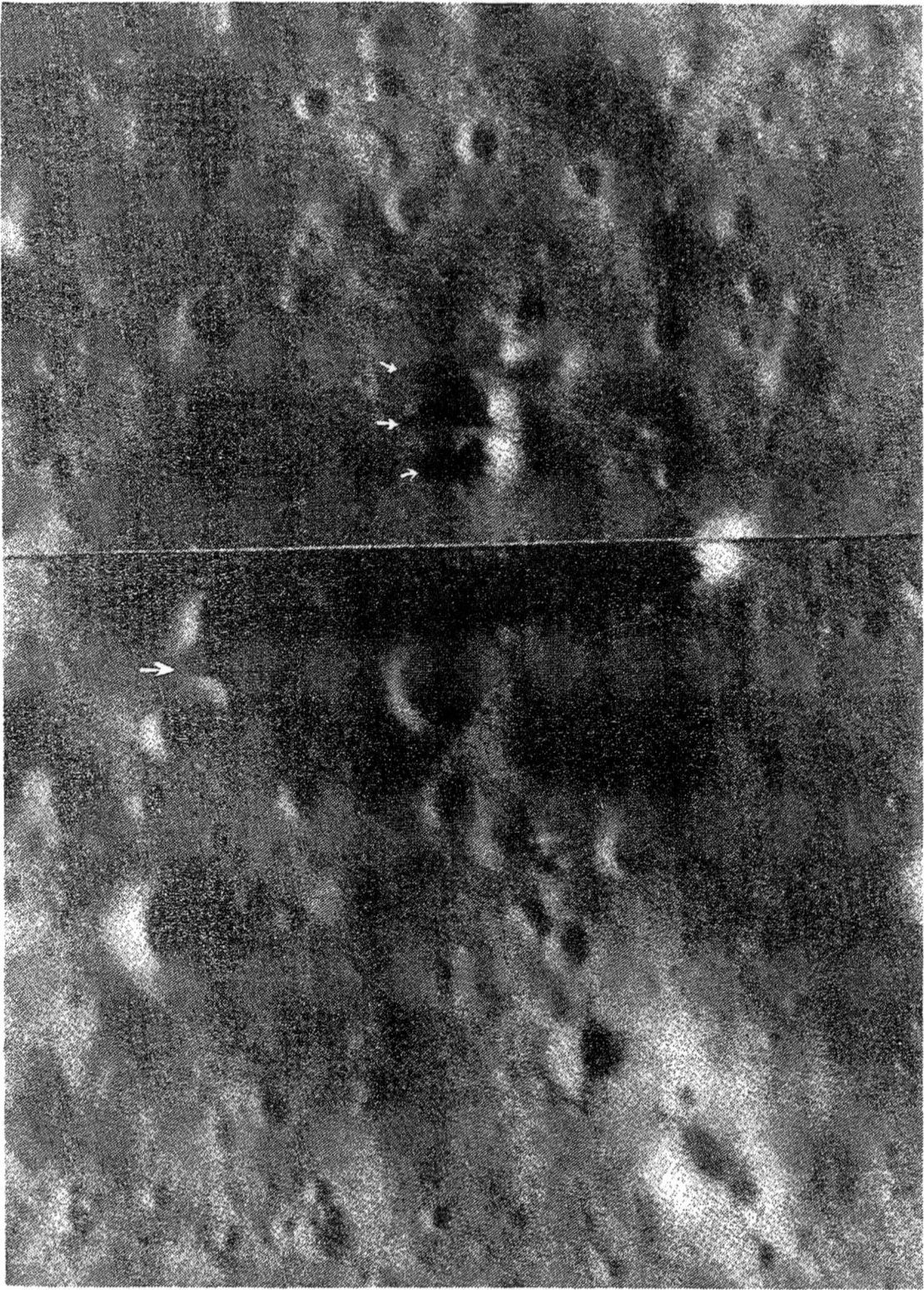

Arrows point to giant pyramid-like objects on moon. The fact that their shadows can be seen indicates that they would have to be of considerable height. Cross can also be seen in crater.

SIGNS OF LIFE

Much information has come to light since the original edition of DANGER ON THE MOON was first released to the public several years ago. Though space probes have come and gone and additional missions have landed on the lunar surface, there is still a feeling among some that the U.S. government is continuing to withhold vital information about the possibility of life on the moon. With the approach of the year 2000 less than two decades away, it appears more than likely that we shall soon meet up with life forms not of this earth. That is if the "powers that be" do not continue to crush all attempts to get this material out to the public. From evidence that we have been shown it could very well be that our astronauts have already established contact with alien beings on the moon, but have been silenced by Uncle Sam.

George Leonard is the author of SOMEBODY ELSE IS ON THE MOON. A free lance writer with many Washington "connections," Leonard long ago released that something "foul" was afoot when it came to NASA's claim that no signs of extraterrestrial intelligence has been found on our nearest neighbor in space. Through personal contacts in the space agency and in other branches of Capitol life, Leonard has been able to put together the pieces of a giant jigsaw puzzle -- a puzzle which confirms our theory that aliens have establish bases on the moon.

The following is a conversation held between George Leonard and UFO REVIEW publisher, Timothy Green Beckley:

BECKLEY: When did you first begin to notice anything strange about the surface of the moon?

LEONARD: It was in the early 1950's. I had home ground telescopes, 6-inch reflectors, and would watch the moon regularly. It was from an older gentleman who knew more about astronomy than I did who first brought my attention to the strange phenomenon taking place there. The thing that would really bug me was the moving patterns of lights. Such lights can't exist on the dark portions of the moon without some sort of intelligence behind them -- yet they were.

BECKLEY: I understand you've gone through hundreds of NASA photos. What have you discovered during this reviewing process?

LEONARD: I've seen gleaming white domes. I've seen tracks of vehicles, beautiful oval objects hovering above the ground. I've also seen gas sprays come up out of a cone and fuzzing the landscape slightly behind it. Also, I've seen what look like old constructions -- shapes that nature doesn't form, and which nature did not build.

BECKLEY: Why can't the average person find these things upon scanning photos taken of the moon during our space shots?

LEONARD: If you look hard enough often you can. I've got some really tremendous photos that NASA released to the British but they never released them in this country.

BECKLEY: Are there instances where there might be something on the moon's surface -- at a particular spot -- and later it will be gone?

LEONARD: About 6 or 8 times I have found what I thought had been some striking change. You have to be very careful in a scientific sense, because if you add light and shadow this can sometimes complicate your viewing. I remember spending two nights until about 4 A.M. trying to clarify what I was seeing. In the end I couldn't be sure because there were too many ifs involved in my observations.

(25)

BECKLEY: Have you ever seen what you thought was a UFO?

LEONARD: In 1952 I was living in Virginia when my wife and I saw something. One evening in April we had parked the car and were looking out over the District when we saw this blue light behind a cloud. The light was shinning down. My wife thought it was a searchlight, but I said it couldn't be because you could see that the light wasn't actually going up from the ground to the cloud, but was coming down through it. When the cloud finally went away the light remained briefly and then it just suddenly went out.

BECKLEY: From your findings, would it be safe to say that the UFOnauts come and go back and forth between the earth and the moon?

LEONARD: I think that it's an odds-on bet that they can come back and forth pretty much at will. From reports of UFOs I've read, they might be making the trip to steal water. A lot of sightings have been made near lakes in Canada and the U.S.

BECKLEY: Do you know of any earth people who have ever been taken to the moon?

LEONARD: I know that earth people have been taken on trips -- I can't say for sure they've been taken to the moon, but that would seem to be a good guess. In ancient times there is evidence that an entire city was taken off the earth. In fact, the "coming and going" might have even been more frequent eons ago. Several cultures had advanced mathematical systems and possessed astronomical data that should not have been known in those days. Some of the structures that were put up centuries past are duplicates of the structures found on the moon. This includes Stonehenge and other similar monuments. This I think is proven by the fact that we have a tribe in Africa called the Cargo Cult who actually build fake airplanes, fake runways because of what they had seen in the sky. Ancient man did the same.

BECKLEY: Has anyone contacted you who is either high up in the government and looking for information, or someone with additional information they are willing to share?

LEONARD: After my book came out I was visited by a congressman and his legal assistant. They spent half a day in my living room and later invited me down to "the hill" to get more data concerning some of the better pictures I had in my possession, and they felt they could ask NASA about. At first I suspected their motives, because often I'm visited by officials who hand me "false leads" in order to throw me off the track. In addition to the congressman and his assistant there was a guy from the army corps of engineers who said he had some things to tell me. He said it didn't feel comfortable talking over the phone, and so I went to his house about two and a half hours away. I spent an entire Saturday there. He showed me slides on his livingroom wall that was given to him by a Major in Denmark. This guy from the Army looked me right in the eye, and said it was all true, that there are lots of pictures that did not get to the public affairs branch of NASA. A few of these I recognized from my own sources, others I did not. One of the slides showed something that alarmed the hell out of me. It was of a spaceship going low over the surface of the moon, and there was what looked like a smoke bomb rising up underneath it casting a beautiful shadow on the ground. The smoke looked like it was coming from between two artificial looking structures. It sure the hell wasn't natural, whatever it was.

BECKLEY: Are there any indications that the Russians know what's going on?

LEONARD: Not only that, but NASA, I believe, is exchanging information with the Soviets. I'm sure of this because I've seen and read many

(26)

documents from the Russians which are written in a language that indicates that there is a great deal of resiprosity going on between our government and their's. There has been much more meshing of data than anyone in NASA will admit. Unlike what we have been made to believe, it has not been a real space race. One time I plotted out all of the Russian and the American space shots to the moon, and it looked like it was our turn to do this, and then their turn to do that.

BECKLEY: Do you think the Russians and the Americans selected particular areas of the moon to land on?

LEONARD: Every manned landing was preceeded by months of careful analysis by NASA and their contractors. They obviously wouldn't want to land while any activity was taking place. That would be like a bull in a china shop. That sort of thing could have caused a confrontation that NASA wouldn't want.

BECKLEY: Have you charted the moon to find out where most of this unusual activity you talk about is taking place?

LEONARD: Tycho is a 60 mile wide crater and this is a real hotbed of activity. This part of the moon looks like a peeled orange. I know for a fact that NASA did an aerial survey of this crater and went to the trouble of blowing the photos up. I've seen some of these shots. They show gleaming white domes all the same size -- a quarter mile in diameter. There are even all kind of tracks going to and fro from this area, perhaps heavy drilling equipment being moved about.

BECKLEY: How long in your estimate have strange things been seen on the moon?

LEONARD: Ever since amateurs started watching the moon. You've got all kinds of stories about long-lasting flares, moving patterns of lights, and craters that disappear within a month. There have even been cases of astronomers seeing light source leaving the moon's surface, and you know its got to be pretty big to be seen through a 6-inch telescope.

BECKLEY: How many sightings would you estimate have been made over the years?

LEONARD: That's really hard to say, but Winnie Campbell of NASA has a collection of almost one thousand, well documented, cases. Patrick Moore has probably more than that. And a guy by the name of Barlett has probably more than both of them put together. Many of these cases have actually come out of scientific journals like NATURE.

BECKLEY: So there is actually reams of available data?

LEONARD: Yes, and NASA has deen doing an overwhelming job lately trying to make people believe that these things are all explainable in natural terms. NASA gives natural reasons, but none of them add up at all.

BECKLEY: I understand that you believe more than one race inhabits the moon. How did you reach this conclusion?

LEONARD: Simply -- I have found what I call "cultural differences." In certain areas, such as the Alpine Valley, there are beautiful domes on sculptured platforms. In other locales there are evidences of gigantic drilling equipment that is responsible for raising the dust all around.

BECKLEY: In all of your research have you uncovered anything which would hint at the fact that the moon might have at one time been a battle ground, and that perhaps this war between interplanetary fractions or groups is still going on?

LEONARD: I mention this bit of speculation in my book...I think it's a good speculation with some suggestive evidence that the moon ran into a horrible calamity. Seismographic sounds indicate that the center of

(27)

Researcher George Leonard

the moon may either be honeycombed or hollow which, in my opinion, would indicate that the moon has been under control of some other group for a long, long time and that maybe -- and this is the key punchline -- the moon eons ago was involved in a gigantic disaster and it had to be pulled into our orbit for a long recuperation and repair jobs. But that's pure speculation.

BECKLEY: You talk about these rigs you claim can be seen in the various craters. Exactly what are these rigs and what are they doing there?

LEONARD: There is one kind of rig that is going around in a spiral as though it were carving out notches down in the crater with laser beams or something. And there's a lot of ruffles (in the photos) because of heavy, fast activity. There's another piece of equipment that stands upright and appears to make deep tracks.

BECKLEY: Can you estimate the size of these rigs?

LEONARD: Between a mile and a mile and a half.

BECKLEY: Why are they doing all this digging?

LEONARD: Possibly they are processing the sand to create oxygen. Earthlings can live for three years on the oxygen that you'd get producing two and a half tons of iron ore -- two and a half tons would keep you alive on the moon in a pressurized dome for three years.

BECKLEY: Would you like to hazard a guess as to what forms of life might be on the moon?

LEONARD: There might be a form of indigenous life that has some sort of root, a conduit going down into the moon for sustenance might exist. Patrick Moore said there might be a form of life on the moon that is far stranger than anything we have ever contemplated. Some of what we have taken to be structures similar to the pyramids might actually

(28)

constitute life forms.

    BECKLEY: What form of life could they be? Seventy feet tall forms of life, or what?

    LEONARD: Does that bother you?

    BECKLEY: Not personally, because they're on the moon and I'm here. It doesn't seem practical.

    LEONARD: It may not seem practical, but don't forget that long, long ago on earth there existed God forsaken creatures a hundred times the size of man. They were so geared to one type of existance that the slightest change in our environment killed them off.

Lunar Orbiter V photographed what George Leonard believes are quarter mile wide domes built by alien forces.

Though George Leonard makes no claims of being a scientist, none-the-less he is a reputable reporter who has authored several books in totally unrelated areas. Leonard is by no means alone in his belief that something pretty strange is taking place on our nearest neighbor in space. Maurice Chatelain is a scientist formerly under contract to the space agency. Chatelain has confessed that when Apollo 11 landed on the moon there were two alien vehicles waiting on a nearby crater rim. The former NASA consultant maintains that several times during their stay on the moon the astronaut's radio transmissions were mysteriously cut off so that they were not broadcast over the airwaves. Chatelain told the NATIONAL ENQUIRER in an exclusive interview that he felt NASA was responsible for the termination because they did not want to let the public know what Neil Armstrong and Buzz Aldrin had come across. Chatelain insists that the astronauts took photos of the extraterrestrial craft. "The pictures have never been published," he confided, "NASA did not release them. They were certainly alien beings there -- but the official record is silent about it."

Dr. Fred Bell in the same ENQUIRER story added these comments: "I've seen photographs of UFOs taken by astronauts -- but when questioned, the astronauts refused to talk about them...The lid has really been clamped down on this." A former consultant to NASA, Dr. Bell believes that the astronauts are trained to keep any UFO encounters a closely guarded secret.

Even more amazing perhaps is the revelation that in the Soviet Union scientists there have for several years been aware of the encounter between our astronauts and alien spacecraft. "I am absolutely certain this episode took place. According to our information the encounter was reported immediately after the landing of the module. Neil Armstrong relayed the message to Mission Control that two large, mysterious objects were watching them after having landed near the moon module. But his message was never heard by the public -- because NASA censored it," or so says Dr. Vladimir Azhazha who the ENQUIRER identifies as a physicist and professor of mathematics at Moscow University.

Additional confirmation that our astronauts have encountered "the unknown" comes from John Schuessler who works at NASA. Schuessler says: "I work with astronauts at NASA and have heard the story from them." Food for thought!

THE DATA COMES IN FROM

ELSEWHERE

The space people themselves have often spoken of their attempts to keep a watchful eye on our various space missions as they fear we earthlings would take our war-like activities to the moon.

Nicholas Faust is an instructor at the June Lake, California based group, the School of Thought, an organization started by the late Hope Troxell, a well known west coast contactee who started receiving channeled messages from extraterrestrials several decades ago. Nicholas recently wrote the UFO REVIEW the follow communication with the express wish that we pass on this information to as many people as possible.

"The extraterrestrials who contacted Mrs.Troxell have often spoken of the U.S. space program which they seem to follow with keen inter-

(30)

est, and they have often commented to us regarding the success or
failures of our astronauts.

"At times, they told us, through the accurate telepathic
receptivity of Mrs. Troxell, that they used a considerable amount of
thought projection on our astronauts (in the upper atmosphere of our
planet and beyond, telepathic receptivity is heightened, even for the
average person). The space people told us that this interpenetration
of thought aided the astronauts considerably helping to insure the
success of the missions aboard the frail Apollo spacecraft.

"It is true, according to the Cosmic Brotherhood of Light, as
they sometimes like to be called, that our astronauts did actually
land on the moon, as reported in the media, but the media only
reported a small and totally non-controversial segment of the
information that was brought back or beamed to us via delayed and
edited television broadcasts from the moon.

"The people of space have told us that the astronauts did indeed
see their spacecraft on the way to and from the moon, as
well as their installations on the moon. However, the astronauts
were forbidden by their seniors from reporting their findings to the
public. A confirmation of the astronauts' secret findings was
given graphically at the last Giant Rock Spacecraft Convention when
one of the speakers showed the audience a series of slides depicting
the space people's installations on the far side of the moon.
These NASA photos, taken by our astronauts orbiting the moon,
were supplied to our NATO allies by our military. They were then borrow-
ed by an officer of the Norwegian military intelligence establishment
and sent back to friends of his who were studying the works of George
Adamski. Needless to say, the photos created quite a bit of interest.

"In a related incident, Mrs. Troxell was given the opportunity
to listen in on the communications between a spacecraft from the
moon and the crew of the almost ill-fated Apollo 13. Apparently Apollo
13 was beginning to tumble out of control after an explosion on board
and the space people came alongside the stricken craft and assisted
the astronauts in re-orientating their small vehicle. At one point,
while the two crafts were flying in formation, the people from the 'Alta
Moon,' as they called themselves, offered to take our astronauts on
board their larger craft, but their offer was politely refused by
the Apollo 13 crew.

"'Gotcha!' was the colloquial term used by the crew of the
'Alta Moon' craft as they began their rendezvous with Apollo 13, and,
interestingly enough, you may remember that one of the later Apollo
Missions nicknamed their lunar rover the 'Gotcha!' I remember watching
Walter Cronkite on CBS news puzzling over the name 'Gotcha!'
for the lunar rover, but if he had known the true story of Apollo 13
the astronauts' choice of the lunar rover's name would be easily
understood."

ESCAPE TO THE MOON

Nicholas Faust says he has strong suspicions that there is a segment of the U.S. government who is planning for the worldwide holocaust
which has been so widely predicted, and will make their escape to the
moon's surface in space ships. "The space people are very indignant
over the fact that those who are the most responsible for the plight
of our world, and the deception of the people, would be those who try
to escape."

(31)

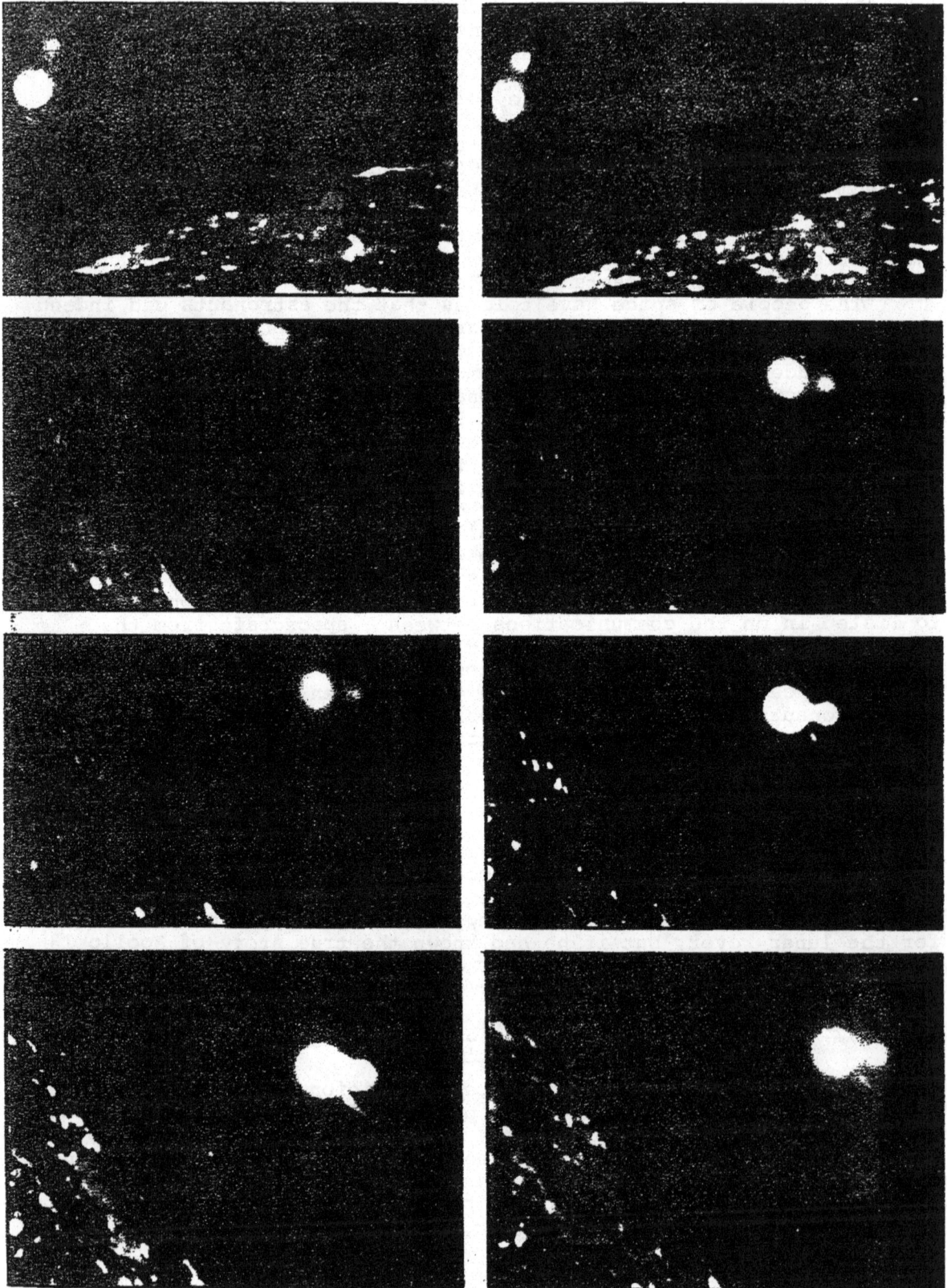

Chinese and other foreign publications printed these photos of UFOs following
our Apollo 11 space mission. NASA never released shots in the United States.

Michael X – Discovers The Nazi Ufo Chronicles by Timothy Green Beckley

If you turn on various cable stations like the History Channel, you are likely to come across several shows dealing with the Nazi development of circular-shaped devices and how members of the German secret society known as the Vril claimed as early as the 1920s to have made contact with interdimensional beings from the stars who gave them the secret of anti gravity propulsion, supplying them with virtual blue prints on how to build a flying saucer. . In my work *Round Trip To Hell In A Flying Saucers* on which I collaborated with many experts in the field including Kenn Thomas, we revealed how the SS sold Hitler on the idea that the Vril society – through a group of nine beautiful female mediums -- had "channeled" technical data from extraterrestrial beings located in the Aldebaran star system.

The existence of World War II flying saucers is a topic which is denied by virtually every reputable authority in aviation history. It is also denied by most self identified "serious UFO researchers" who have not concerned themselves with spending ten minutes studying the German saucer story. In the years immediately following the Second World War the earth's skies suddenly began to be populated by flying craft capable of performing some remarkable tasks. They flew at unheard of speeds. They made very sharp turns, seemingly non-aerodynamic turns, even at this extreme speed. They lacked the glowing tail of jets or rockets, but they glowed or gave off light at night from their periphery or from the whole craft. They were mostly silent . Sometimes they gave off sounds that an electric generator or motor might make. Sometimes vehicles with electrically based ignition systems ceased to operate in the presence of these saucers. No government claimed these flying craft, yet they were seen all over the planet.

The press and popular culture attributed these unusual craft to an extraterrestrial source. It seem to be the simplest solution to the mystery at hand. Yet, after over seventy five years now no conclusive proof can be given for their point of origin or origins. Some are obviously a form of psychic manifestation or a product of a "supernatural force" like the Jinn. Others appear to be quite solid and capable of leaving indentions in the soul and taking selected humans on board for conversation and a ride or two helter skelter style through the cosmos.

It seems only proper to begin searching for an explanation for field propulsion saucers with the very sources which we now know built conventional flying saucers, the Germans of the Third Reich. Now hold onto your twirling beanies for all intense and purposes the earliest reference to a field propulsion German made flying saucer is from a 1960 book by Michael X in which it is described as a "flying egg." Later around 1968, Michael X also wrote *The German Saucer Story*. The second book returns to the theme again, this time citing a confidential source. His primarily informant being Hermann Klaas, who describes to Michael X a dozen secret Nazi weapons, which include:

1. The flying disc
2. A tank made entirely of one piece of metal
3. The sound wave weapon
4. A laser beam weapon
5. A flaming artificial cloud
6. A robot bomb
7. A charged cloud weapon
8. An armor piercing projectile
9. The electromagnetic KM-2 rocket
10. A paralyzing ray
11. Electronic ball lighting
12. The flying bottle, tube, sphere, etc.

Apparently following the close of WWII, the forerunners of the CIA, the OSI were happy to bring Nazi war criminals to the U.S. as long as they could continue to upgrade and produce their horrendous weapons which could be turned against the Soviet Union and others during the Cold War. This kept the war machine running full blast in the United States.

Here we have Michael X's initial writing on the earthly constructed German flying discs. Its far to late to quiver over whether Hitler escaped his German bunker for South America,' though if Michael X was right about the German built flying saucers, it is certainly possible he knew what he was talking about when it came to Hitler leaving Germany under the cloak of darkness.

I believe the crash at Roswell was of a German made craft. After all what sort of technology came from the downed crashed disc that would be ten thousand years advanced from what we had already developed on earth? Tin foil that could unfold and smooth itself back into its original shape? A craft so light and constructed of parts that appeared to be made of balsa wood? There isn't anything here to prove that extraterrestrials were involved. The bodies came later as an afterthought, which could well have been dummies – real dummies. I have worked on enough movie sets and seen what a master special effects maker is capable of creating when it comes to making the living look dead, or the dead living for that matter. The rule of thinking among the CIA seems to have been "the public be damned, but if they have to believe in flying saucers and little green men lets make them think they come from Mars or beyond. . . and not Nazi Germany!"

Also, in a lot of the early UFO reports from the late 1940s and 50s, the saucer pilots spoke with a decisively German accent. Ask Reinhold O. Schmidt the Nebraska grain buyer who was invited inside a saucer-shaped device and who carried on a dialogue with the pilot of the craft, where he thinks they might have originated from if he were being truthful. And why did the German scientists who "escaped" to America under Project Paperclip set up shop in New Mexico home to several UFO crashes and lots of UFO sightings toward the end of 40s? Pure coincidence? And hey, how about the saucer pilots themselves observed around UFOs that had been seen to land? On many occasions, these saucer pilots – the aliens if you want to call them that -- were said to be tall, blue eyed and blond haired. Sounds like the prototype for Hitler's Arian race I would say. German actors with spaceship garb perhaps handed out by the CIA or other top notch officials who wanted to give the impression that all saucer pilots were beguine so that we would embrace them with open arms, while the real "bad apples' went on with their clandestine operations? It is important you do your own thinking in this regard.

But let us not get ahead of ourselves. Instead let us allow our good friend Michael X fill in the missing details – as much, anyway, as was known at the time he published this little known monograph on Hitler's escape and the construction of Nazi flying saucers.

We Want You- UFO, Hitler Connection by Michael X

Original Title:
We Want You – Is Hitler Alive?

We Want You!

by

Michael X

THIS is an Educational and Inspirational Book of Study especially written and intended for NEW AGE individuals als everywhere. It contains Seven fascinating chapters. Statements in this Book are based on Scientific, Super sensory and Personal findings of the author. No claim is made as to what the information cited might do in any given case, and the Publishers assume no obligation for the opinions expressed or implied here by the author.

▲

FOREWORD

THE MYSTERY OF UFO's -- Unidentified
Flying Objects -- is the greatest mystery
of our age, and it has many facets. Like
a gigantic jig-saw puzzle, the missing parts
must be put into place in order for the picture to make complete sense. You and I are
adventuring together and finding valuable
missing parts along the roadside.

In this unusual adventure we shall explore the facet of Nazi-built UFO's. Adolph
Hitler, as we might suspect, enters the picture as a part of the UFO mystery. Not all,
but a definite part of it.

Michael Nostradamus, the French Seer,
is also a part of this amazing drama, for
he predicted that Hitler would escape from
his enemies at the end of World War II.
This event, as you will shortly see, has
already happened. But more important to
you and me and the world is the question:
Will the Nazis return to the world scene in
Earth-built UFO's?

Before we begin this great new adventure, let me once again bolster your faith
in the existence of INTERPLANETARY space
ships and visitors from other planets.
They are real. In space progress, some
planets are far, far ahead of our little
world. My conviction -- based on personal
experiences -- is that our planet has had
many visitations by highly evolved beings.
They are still watching us.

But not all UFO's are true space ships.
Not all come from outside -- or inside --
our planet Earth. Some of them are built
on this Earth by secret forces on Earth.
It now appears that "they" possess the secret of a POWER that may well be the key to
the FATE of the world. That is why it is
so vital that we learn something about "them"
and their motives.

THIS is the inside story of the Nazi
UFO's.

MICHAEL X

* * *

TRILOGY OF THE UNKNOWN
IS ADOLPH HITLER ALIVE?

Chapter One

Since 1951 I have been following with great interest, the unfoldment of a strange and remarkable prediction. It concerns one of history's most vital questions, namely : <u>Is Adolph Hitler alive?</u>

A most gifted forecaster of future events -- Michael Nostradamus -- envisioned a leader escaping from those who wanted to kill him. I believe that the man whom Nostradamus saw in his vision, was none other than the Nazi leader, Adolph Hitler. And thereon hangs a most unusual and fascinating story.

With uncanny power, Nostradamus could look far into future time by means of "ESP" -- Extra-Sensory Perception. What he saw happening in our own time -- the 20th Century -- is incredible. He foresaw the advent of Hitler upon the world scene. Furthermore, the gifted Seer left certain "quatrains" or verses, for us to read, which clearly describe Adolph Hitler.

But the most IMPORTANT prophetic verse Nostradamus wrote regarding Hitler, is the one that tells HOW Hitler <u>escaped death</u>. Why is this so important? You will, I am sure, fully understand why, as you proceed more deeply with me into this mystery. As the saying goes, there is "more to this than meets the eye". There is a significance to the event of Hitler's escape, and so it is not simply that we are curious about one man, but whether or not those FORCES which he represented, are still <u>active</u> in our world.

Here then, is the amazing "escape" of Hitler as the French Seer, Nostradamus, saw it and revealed it to mankind:

> "The leader who shall lead
> an infinite number of people,
>   Far from their homeland to
> one of strange manners and
>   language,
> Five thousand in Candia and
>   Thessaly finished,
> The leader escaping, shall be
>   safe in a barn on the sea."

As you read this verse over quietly two or three times, you notice that it indeed seems to be describing (in a veiled way of course) the mysterious fate of the one-time Nazi boss of all Germany.

- 3 -

To give us the idea more emphatically that it was a submarine that Hitler used for his escape from the Allies at the end of World War II, Nostradamus wrote another verse:

"Wild beasts for hunger shall swim
    over the rivers,
Most of the land affected shall be
    near the Danube.
Into an iron cage he shall cause the
    great one to be drawn,
When the child of Germany shall
    observe nothing."

Meaning? Could it be that Nostradamus was seeing in his mind's eye a vision of proud and noble Germany beaten to her knees in the closing days of the war? Here is the picture:

Berlin has fallen to the Allies. All is dark despair, hunger, and hopelessness for the Germans. A report has gone out to the people to the effect that Hitler, Eva Braun, Joseph Goebbels and his family have all "committed suicide" -- are dead.

But was that report true? No. Nostradamus saw no suicide of the Nazi leader nor of those who were with him in the Bunker at Berlin during the final hours. If not suicide, then....what?

Escape. Get-away! How? By means of an "iron cage" -- a submarine --in a manner so clever, so well planned that not even the Germans themselves suspected! Adolph Hitler was alive!

Things are not always what they seem to be. If we let ourselves judge only from "appearances" we are sure to be fooled. According to the general report, it appeared that Hitler had died by his own hand on May 1, 1945. I am convinced he did not.

I believe that Hitler escaped death...that he is alive today. His purported "suicide" was not a fact, but a great hoax. Of that we are quite certain. For the evidence you are about to read is not based on mere conjectures but on indisputable facts.

Are you ready for bold adventure? Adventure of world-wide importance in which we push back new frontiers? Then come...

4

First of all, it is important for us to realize that the assumed death of Adolph Hitler is something that neither the highest diplomat in America nor England nor Russia believes. Why? And why did Dwight D. Eisenhower publicly state on June 15th, 1945, that he had "grave doubts about the certainty" of Hitler's death?

Was it because of what American Intelligence officers failed to find in the "Fuehrerbunker" of Adolph Hitler? It was in this Bunker -- underground fortress of the Nazi Chancellory -- that the Allies searched for Hitler's remains. The story is this:

Hitler was supposed to have died of bullet wounds...death by suicide. His body was then supposedly doused with gasoline which was ignited so that the body was "cremated". The ashes? They were reportedly buried somewhere in the Chancellory yard.

But what are the facts?

Inside the Bunker the Americans found some blood stains but they were not of Hitler's type.

Outside in the garden, our intelligence technicians were just as unlucky. They found not a single bone, not even a tooth, no ashes, nothing that backed up in even the smallest way the story of Hitler's purported "suicide and cremation".

At once the Americans realized the glaring truth. Hitler's death was a great hoax...a lie. He had somehow staged the whole thing to fool his enemies. But his enemies were not fooled. Not the Americans. And if Marshal Zhukov, the conquering general from Russia, was fooled , his words didn't indicate it.

"The circumstances of Hitler's death," Zhukov stated, "are very mysterious. We have not identified the body of Hitler. I can say nothing about his fate. He could have flown away from Berlin at the very last moment. The condition of the runway would have allowed him to."

What did General Zhukov mean when he said that "very mysterious circumstances" were connected with Hitler's fate? At the official investigation carried out by Zhukov and his intelligence men, suspicious facts came to light.

5

When the Russians questioned the witnesses they had captured at the Bunker, the truth came out. The witnesses revealed that they had sworn to Hitler that if ever they fell into the hands of the enemy, they would maintain that they had seen his body and Eva Braun's body burning.

"In reality, " the Russians quote them as confessing, "We never saw either bodies or any live coals!"

The Russian investigators further stated that when their detachments came to the Chancellory garden on May 2, they found the charred bodies of Joseph Goebbels and his wife, and the burned bodies of their six children. They could find no trace of Hitler and Eva Braun. Nor did they locate any spot where they were supposed to have been cremated. One thing, however, was seen.

A jawbone with teeth. The Russians at once tried to locate Hitler's dentist. Oddly enough, both the dentist and his wife had completely disappeared. The "assistant dentist" identified the jawbone and teeth as "belonging to Hitler". But did it?

The jawbone could have been "planted" at the Bunker by the Nazis just before the Fuehrer made his escape. It is logical to assume that both the head dentist and his assistant were Nazis, and that the head dentist and his wife joined Hitler's get-away group. At any rate, they are still missing.

"We have established irrefutably, " the Russian report says, "that at dawn of April 30 a small plane carrying three men and a woman took off from the Tiergarten. Hitler's personal pilots -- Baur and Beetz -- have disappeared. Neither we nor the Americans have ever found them."

Another Russian commander echoed Zhukov. "We have found several bodies that might be Hitler's, but we cannot state that he is dead. My opinion is that Hitler has gone into hiding somewhere in Europe, possibly with General Franco."

Although it might seem obvious, Hitler could not have sought refuge in Europe. Much too risky. Neither could he have escaped

6

to one of the neutral countries such as Switzerland. Had any Government been so foolish as to provide a safe haven for Hitler, the act would have brought down the full wrath of the great powers upon it. It would have caused further bloody conflict, ending no doubt, in Hitler's capture.

We must bear in mind that Hitler was considered "World Criminal No. 1" by the Allied nations. Even under a disguise, some alert agent would have very quickly spotted him.

Frequently there have been rumors that German submarines, during their wartime travels to strange and remote places, had discovered an ideal refuge for the Fuehrer. There are tales about Hitler's "Castle on the Baltic", his "Fortress in the Rhineland", his "Monastery hide-out in Spain", his "Stronghold in Albania".

I have even heard a rumor that Hitler is being held a prisoner secretly by British intelligence on a small island off the coast of Scotland. The evidence, however, now indicates that all those stories are but wild tales. Yet Hitler did escape successfully.

Then where did he and his submarine convoy go in order to find a secure hiding place from which to resume activities, and plan future moves? It had to be away from the continent of Europe. And it could not be an island -- too tiny -- not enough growing room to expand into a large and powerful organized force.

Where did he go? Does any land exist where both climate and conditions for development are suitable? Does a land exist that is not overly populated and big enough to discourage enemies?

Yes, such a land exists. It is a big land, terribly big. It is located far from the continent of Europe. And its very remoteness makes it an ideal "haven of refuge" for Hitler and his group.

★★★★★★★

7

Chapter 2

In the previous chapter we had established a startling fact
-- Adolph Hitler, leader of the Nazi Party in Germany -- did not
die in the Bunker when the Allies invaded Berlin in 1945. How
then, did he escape? And where did he go?

According to the prophecy of Nostradamus, Hitler used a submarine for his daring escape. Why then, did the Russian report
mention that a small plane had been seen taking off from the
Tiergarten runway, in the cold dawn of April 30th? The answer
to this question is that Hitler made use of both the plane and
the submarine to accomplish his successful get-away.

At the Bunker where Hitler and his companions staged the
big hoax of "suicide and cremation", there were a number of underground passages leading in every direction. One of the passages led to the vicinity of the airport runway.

In the Bunker with Hitler were Eva Braun, and four important
men of the Nazi Party. Martin Bormann (Hitler's right hand man
and brilliant organizer), Eric Kempa, General Von Greim, and
Joseph Goebbels with his wife and six children. They all escaped
with the exception of Goebbels and his family.

Why did Goebbels die? There are two possibilities we may
consider. One: Goebbels and family might have escaped with
the others, and left doubles in their places. All the bodies
when found were charred beyond recognition. Two: Goebbels might
have turned traitor which could have caused the Nazis to shoot
him. There is good reason to believe this is so.

Although Joseph Goebbels was a genius at the art of propa-
ganda, he apparently had no real love for the German people.
Curt Riess, the writer who did a Biography of Goebbels, pointed
out that "his contempt for the German people shocked fellow
Nazis."   And the Nazis weren't easily shocked!

- 8 -

But didn't Joseph Goebbels worship Hitler, and build up the prestige of the Fuehrer? Yes, at first. But Biographer Riess found that in the end Goebbels hated Hitler and even treated him as an imbecile instead of a God.

It is more than probable that Hitler and his entourage did not depend upon a single small plane to make their escape from the Bunker. Nor did they all leave on the same day. More than one get-away planes were no doubt employed by the escapees, and it is a good bet they left long before the "last minute".

The Nazi leader and his companions flew to a small port in Norway. It was there they kept a carefully planned "rendezvous" with a top-secret convoy of German U-boats. There -- sometime between April 22nd and May 2nd, 1945, -- Hitler and his aides embarked on the submarine that was to take them into the South Atlantic en route to a mystery destination.

The silent convoy of U-boats headed southward, following the "flagship" commanded by Admiral Karl Doenitz. It was his task to lead the convoy of submarines to the already prepared refuge which awaited them. Doneitz, in fact, had helped to plan the escape. He knew all about the secret "Shangri-La" Hideout.

When Hitler made his "last will and testament" he appointed the new German Nazi Government. Admiral Karl Doenitz was to become Reich President. Joseph Goebbels was to become Reich Chancellor, and Martin Bormann was to be Party Minister.

Most unusual! Why was Doenitz scheduled to become President of the Reich? Why not some politician, or Army general, or Airforce man? Why was a Navy man selected by Hitler?

Because Hitler was counting heavily upon Doenitz with his U-boats to assist him to escape alive from the danger area..and only an underwater submarine convoy could do this! U-boats in the German fleet were extremely difficult to detect, inasmuch as they traveled deeply submerged nearly all of the time.

9

ADMIRAL DOENITZ

Proof that Admiral Doenitz made the necessary arrangements by which Hitler escaped to a safe refuge, is not difficult to find. Doenitz, in the year 1943, let the "cat out of the bag" by saying: "The German submarine fleet is proud of having built for the Fuehrer in another part of the world, a Shangri-La on land, an impregnable fortress!"

The world quickly forgot this unusual statement by Doenitz in those hectic wartime days that followed. It was, however, most revealing. An impregnable fortress -- a Hideout -- had been built for Adolph Hitler in a land that was a veritable "Shangri-La"!

Where? South America -- tropical and warm -- huge in area and far enough away to discourage enemies, was the selected land. Argentina was the particular province that was chosen.

As early as 1948 it was suspected that Hitler had fled to Argentina in a submarine especially outfitted for that purpose. The Biographer, Curt Riess, in his book about Joseph Goebbels, was the first one (to my knowledge) to mention this astounding idea.

Two years later, in 1950, Gerald K. Smith backed up the big rumor. Speaking to a large audience at the University of Tulsa in Tulsa, Oklahoma, Smith not only claimed that Adolph Hitler was alive...but gave names of prominent persons who had seen and spoken to Hitler in Buenos Aires, Argentina!

In 1951-52, the editors of "The National Police Gazette" had gathered a mountain of evidence to the effect that the deposed Nazi leader was hiding in Argentina. A series of articles under the title: "Hitler Is Alive!" was published by that Magazine.

Those early articles told of the strange series of events that happened shortly after Hitler's supposed death. Unfortunately, back issues of The Police Gazette in which the full story appeared, are no longer obtainable. But here is the gist of it:

10

TRILOGY OF THE UNKNOWN

Strange but true, the German submarine U-530 had entered into the Argentine port of Mar del Plata on July 10, 1945. There it had surrendered to the Argentine officials.

Seven days later, on July 17, 1945, a second German sub entered Mar del Plata and also surrendered. It was identified as the U-977. The crew of both the U-530 and U-977 were questioned by the U.S. authorities, but the results of the questioning were never made public. They remain in the closed files of the Secret Service agencies, labeled, no doubt: TOP SECRET.

This strange fact is known. Both of the submarines contained surprisingly large food stores on board. There was a food supply sufficient enough to last for three, maybe four months at sea without restocking the larder. And both subs had been in the high seas for several months...on some unknown mission.

What were those submarines doing at Argentina? Why were they prowling around in the Atlantic even after the war ended? Clearly, they were part of the "mystery convoy" that transported Hitler, his aides and their personal valuables from war-wrecked Berlin to the new "Shangri-La" -- Argentina, South America!

"The Police Gazette" in December 1960, released to its reading public new, positive proof of Hitler's escape. The article was written by George McGrath, and titled : "HITLER IN ARGENTINA". It presents irrefutable new information on the Hitler mystery. By all means secure a copy of this new article in The Police Gazette at once...while they last. Address is : H.H. Roswell, Publisher, The National Police Gazette, 250 West 57th St. New York 19, N.Y. When you write, enclose a stamp, and ask how much the Dec.1960 back issue will cost per copy.

In the above mentioned article, Mr. McGrath reports that he personally has examined documents in the files of Allied intelligence authorities. They confirm Hitler's escape. McGrath says that the startling new revelations about Hitler have been verified by the highest counter-espionage sources.

Adolph Hitler, then, is in Argentina. Why -- if that is so -- haven't the U.S. authorities gone in and captured him? For several very good reasons. For one thing, Argentina is known

11

to be "pro-Nazi". Former dictator Peron of Argentina was a very strong fascist and a good friend of Hitler. In fact, the Fuehrer has many friends and protectors in the Argentine government. By not cooperating with Allied intelligence agents, they shield him.

Then too, it is well-nigh impossible for any CIA (Central Intelligence Agency) men to get into Hitler's stronghold. Doenitz had boasted it was "an impregnable fortress". It is no doubt, exactly that. And according to McGrath's information, Hitler's "stronghold" is guarded by armed Germans.

The Hideout is located somewhere in "Patagonia". Patagonia is that area of Argentina where the Germans are particularly well-entrenched. Not only did the Nazis move their own people out of Germany, but millions of dollars as well. Fantastic as it may seem now, some $750 million dollars of Nazi wealth was funneled out of Germany into Argentina late in the war.

Using those funds, Admiral Doenitz and other top Nazis purchased many thousands of square miles of ranchland in Patagonia. The vast, sprawling acres known as "Pampas" were bought up and converted into the new, secret headquarters of the Nazis.

Aside from the fact that Hitler's Hideout is guarded by armed men, it would still be unwise for the Allies to attempt to capture Hitler and take him back for trial. His capture would undoubtedly lead to international complications of the most alarming kind... We shall soon see why this is so. Why Hitler is "too hot to handle". And why the U.S. makes no attempt to touch him now.

Please give your closest attention to what I am about to say. It is new and startling information. I ask you to keep this information in strictest confidence. It is for mature minds only.

LISTEN! Inside the "Sanctum Sanctorum" of the Hitler forces in Patagonia, what do you imagine you and I would find, if we were permitted to travel unmolested past the gates of the Hideout? Would we, dear friend, meet with the surprise of our lifetime ? Would we come upon certain underground installations - factories - staffed by German scientists ? There for what purpose?

To design, build and test what we would call "UFO's"!

★★★★★★★

12

CHAPTER 3

The Circle-Wing Craft

———————•———————

During the war the Nazis under Adolph Hitler authorized and carried out many secret military projects. Thousands of German scientists were set to work on these projects. This secret work was done at Peenemunde Island, Germany, and at other hidden centers underground. Two of these underground "factories" were located near Nordhaussen and Bleicherode, another at Traunstein, Germany. Each factory was given a secret "code name".

In charge of these secret projects were Professor Werner Von Braun, Professor Herman Oberth, and other missile experts. The designs for V-type rockets came from their drawing boards. For example, the V-1 and V-2 guided rockets which the Nazis used with such telling effect during the war.

SCHAUBERGER AND THE SILENT SAUCER

Now, dear friend, read on. For we are coming to a most significant "turn of events". Of all the secret inventions of World War II, by far the most exciting was the one that came out of Bad Ischl, Germany, as early as 1940. Around that time, a very brilliant engineer -- Vikton Schauberger -- was experimenting with Diamagnetism. That is, Schauberger was testing the attracting and repulsing properties of materials such as copper and various alloys. The results of his experiments were excellent.

Schauberger built model-size "saucer-shaped" craft for his tests. Some were bell-shaped, some hat-shaped. He powered them with an "Electro-Magnetic" engine of his own design. By means of this new type of propulsion -- Electro-Magnetism -- The inventor succeeded in causing the disc-shaped models to fly silently through the air. And ... wonder of wonders ...the new Electro-Magnetic drive motor was flameless and smokeless!

13

Schaubergers Versuchsmodelle von fliegenden Scheiben aus Kupfer.
Gebaut im Jahre 1940 bei Fa. Kertl in Wien IV.

SCHAUBERGER'S EXPERIMENTAL MODEL OF A FLYING SAUCER
MADE FROM COPPER.   BUILT IN 1940 BY KERTL CO. IN VIENNA..

In the June 1957 issue of URANUS, editor Egerton Sykes wrote:
"Engineer Vikton Schauberger of the Biological Institute of Bad
Ischl, well known for his 'Golden Plough' and his water purifica-
tion system, is reported to have produced and flown, as far back
as 1940, hat or bell-shaped craft -- presumably of model sizes --
made from copper utilizing diamagnetism. A reference to this is
in Mr. Sievers' book, Flying Saucers Over SouthAfrica."

Note that carefully..."produced and flown" in 1940. Where?
In Germany, and during the very time Adolph Hitler was in power.
We can safely assume that the Fuehrer's secret service agents --
who didn't miss a trick -- were fully aware of engineer Vikton
Schauberger's fabulous invention: the silent UFO.

14

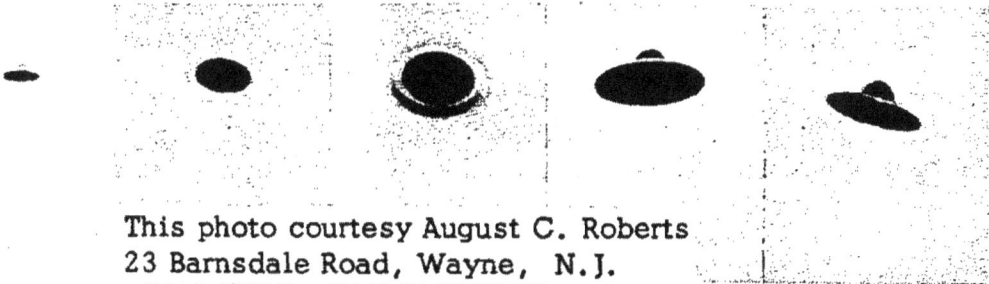

This photo courtesy August C. Roberts
23 Barnsdale Road, Wayne, N.J.

(Above) In 1952, George J. Stock of Passaic, N.J., took five photos in sequence of same UFO as it passed over his home. Note force-field around the UFO. Also note striking resemblance to Schauberger craft shown in lower picture. It is "hat-shaped".

(Below) In 1940, Vikton Schauberger of Germany, built this "hat-shaped" model flying machine. It flew by "Electro-Magnetic" power which produced a force-field. Conclusion: UFO above could be a German-built device.

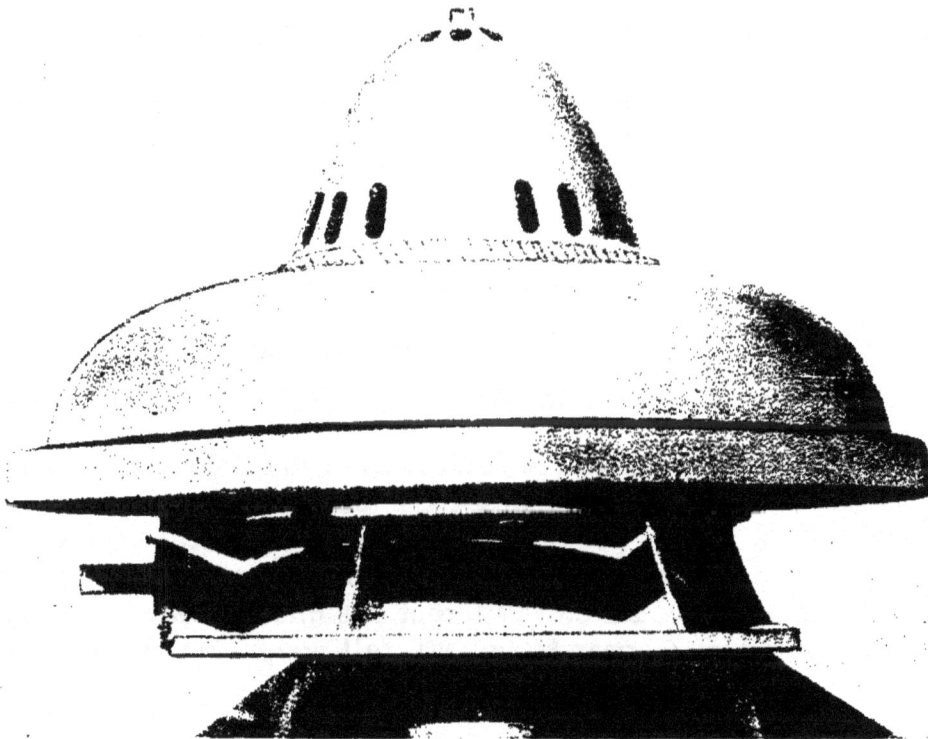

15

By 1943 Admiral Doenitz of the Nazi submarine fleet had not only located the ideal "Hideout" for the Fuehrer in far-off Patagonia, but had started furnishing that fortress lavishly. All the essential men, machines, buildings, laboratories, factories, tools, secret protective devices, everything Doenitz could find went into the "Shangri-La" Nazi project.

Including Vikton Schauberger's blueprints. Schauberger himself, did not leave Germany. But the plans for his invention of the "silent UFO" were far too precious to be overlooked by the Nazi secret agents. Doubtless they delivered a full set of the invention plans to the scientific technicians in Patagonia. As for the fate of Schauberger, I am told that he was set upon by mysterious assailants in 1952. He was badly injured in the chest and died three months later. A sad end for a genius.

Adolph Hitler always wanted "super-weapons". He knew that what he lacked in man-power he had to make up for by means of advanced science and technology. Prior to war's end in 1945, he pulled every conceivable string to get guided rocket missiles into production. He even had in mind a mammoth rocket -- the V-10 -- with a 5,000 mile range. And he had his eye on Schauberger's amazing invention. It required very little imagination to see how the Circle-Wing Craft, if perfectly silent and unbelievably fast, could be the means of winning the war.

Are you ready for more suprises? Good! Hold onto your hat because action gets more intense from here on.

In June, 1960, a German friend of mine -- whose name must remain confidential -- added another "missing part" to the great jig-saw puzzle. This friend stated that during the war he had acquaintance with Germans in East Prussia. They admitted to him that there were secret UNDERGROUND FACTORIES in the East Prussian forests, which produced key parts of the V-1 and V-2.

Not only that. Experiments were also made there on strange "ellipse-shaped" or "egg-shaped" metallic air-craft. In other words, Hitler was in possession of enough technical "know-how" regarding the new principle of propulsion (electro-magnetism) to apply it to crafts of several different designs. Now turn to the next page and my German friend will tell you of his experience:

16

HERE IS THE INSIDE STORY

"In Schramberg, South Bavaria, I had a friend who's father was a renowned Metallurg scientist. He experimented with the chemistry of metals. There is little doubt but that he was one of the world's most brilliant minds, for it was this same scientist who invented <u>a metal harder than diamonds</u>. In 1935-36 the Nazis put this amazing metal -- we shall call it IMPERVIUM -- to use for the first time in airplanes of the German Air Force.

"I recall visiting his fantastic laboratories under a luxurious house at Lake Schramberg. He allowed me to see how the metal glowed with a red-blue florescence when heated to a high degree.

"One year later (in the 1940's) I met this scientist and his daughter again, this time at the Polish Embassy. The daughter told me that her father had been called for an audience with Hitler that very night. The scientist's consultation with Hitler concerned secret plans for an OVAL or 'ELLIPSE-SHAPED' aircraft."

<u>AUTHOR'S COMMENT</u>: From this data it appears the Nazis were definitely building an "egg-shaped" mystery ship, a top-secret UFO. Its source of power for flight? Electro-magnetism or "electrified propulsion system". Its chassis built with heat-resistant metal: IMPERVIUM, the metal harder than diamonds!

I believe that manufacture of these egg-shaped UFO's and Circle-Wing Craft began in Germany's underground factories, but was moved to Argentina when military defeat appeared certain. How, one asks, could Hitler's Third Reich -- on the verge of collapse -- finance such a project? And in Argentina! Nothing is more costly than research and the manufacturing of strange, new types of secret flying machines in some far distant land!

* * * * * *

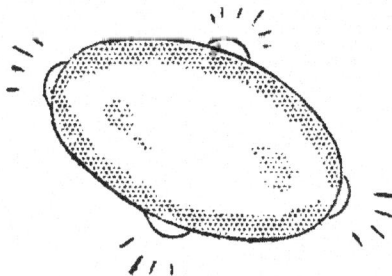

- 17 -

CHAPTER 4

His Hand Reaches Back

◆

In 1942 the Fuehrer needed money and plenty of it. He needed money to research and develop "Super Weapons" with which to win the war. He needed money to expand his operations in South America, at the "Stronghold". He also required a large supply of money in case Germany lost the victory.

Hitler was advised that the quickest way to make money is to "make" money. During a war there is certainly no time to "earn" big money. It had to be "made-to-order" -- counterfeited.

The code name for this fantastic counterfeiting plan was "Operation Bernhard". Using this secret code name for their "money-making" operations, the Nazis manufactured $600,000,000 of British bank notes in World War II. This money was so perfectly counterfeited it was impossible to tell it from the genuine article.

"Operation Bernhard" is one of the most fascinating reports to come out of World War II. It is still labeled SECRET in the files of American, British, French and German intelligence agencies. INTERPOL which is the International Criminal Police Organization in Paris, has carbons of the report in its files. Operation Bernhard was big. Biggest in fact, of any counterfeiting activity of all time. And at the head of it was Adolph Hitler.

You can now learn all the inside details concerning Hitler's amazingly ingenious set up that turned out so much bogus British money...details which we have not space for here. It is all revealed in a small, paper-back pocket book entitled: MONEY OF THEIR OWN, by Murray Teigh Bloom. The book sells for 50¢. If your bookstore cannot supply you, a copy can be obtained direct from Ballantine Books, Inc., 101 Fifth Ave., New York 3, N.Y. I'm sure you would enjoy reading its fascinating facts.

18

One of those facts is that late in August of 1943, a leading member of the Nazi Party took $250,000,000 worth of the bogus bank notes with him to South America. There it was used, as we have previously mentioned, to "buy up" great tracts of land in Argentina, namely Patagonia.

Hitler's "Shangri-La" fortress cost money. Not only was it necessary to purchase land, it was also urgently required -- money that is -- to enable the German scientists to continue building the first working models of Hitler's "mystery weapons".

Money -- "made-to-Hitler's order" -- kept pouring into Patagonia via well established Nazi channels. The "impregnable fortress" became more and more luxuriously appointed. More important, progress on hhe secret UFO's (the Circle-Wing and Oval Shaped Craft) zoomed ahead. Hitler was optimistic.

But things were not going so well in Germany. 1944 saw things looking worse than ever before for the Nazis. By early 1945 they saw the "handwriting on the wall". Hitler's engineers had not managed to come up with the super weapons in time, and the Allies were preparing to storm Berlin. Hitler gave the order for a special run of the counterfeit money. Operation Bernhard in Berlin was to run off $10,000,000 (ten million dollars) of British pound notes. It was to be used by the Nazi leaders in Germany, as "getaway money"!

The special order got immediate attention. Result? Several thousands of top Nazis left Germany. The escape route was to Spain, and from there by boat to Argentina, South America.

Suddenly the war was over. The Allies had won, and it was taken for granted by the general public that the story of Adolph Hitler's "suicide" was true. It was not. Hitler was simply not the suicide kind of individual. Far from it!

Herr Keitel, the Nazi Chief of Staff, reported that the Fuehrer was something of a health fanatic. He went for a walk in the woods every morning while in his command post in the Black Forest. And how about Hitler's diet? It was strange indeed as compared with that of his fellow officers. Hitler did not eat meat. And it was widely known that he fasted from all solid foods at

19

least three successive days a month.

Now dear friend, considering the above, it is highly unlikely -- if not impossible -- that a man who looked after his physical condition to that degree would destroy himself. It is far more likely that Hitler -- who considered himself a man of Destiny -- would include himself in the Nazi getaway plans!

Hitler, far from being dead, is most probably very much alive. Quite naturally, he'd be older now...somewhere in his early seventies. But calendar years, we must remember, are not at all the important thing to one who "takes care of himself" properly. It's biological years, not calendar years that slow a man down.. make him weak and ineffectual. Right?

In my opinion -- take it for what it is worth to you -- I'd say Adolph Hitler is in good physical health today. I believe he has been diligently "planning big things" ever since he was forced to vacate Germany and flee to his "Shangri-La".

Those plans involve a resumption of power, obviously. But I think there is more to it than that. Hitler's birthdate was April 20, 1889. Those who know something of Astrology would say Hitler was born "on the cusp" between Aries and Taurus. That gives him a blending of qualities from both signs, Aries and Taurus. Result? Almost unbelievable boldness, daring, energetic drive. Such a person demands power, great power...yet has an uncanny ability to wield it. He can both gain and use POWER,

And here are the amazing facts. From his Hideout, the Fuehrer seems to be directing the rebirth of Nazi Germany. The hand of Hitler is reaching back . And it is beginning to touch and reorganize present-day modern Germany.

Germany today, as you know, is divided into West and East sectors. East Germany is controlled by the Russians, so it is in West Germany that Nazilsm is being "revived". Not that the West German Government approves. It is only too aware of what "Nazi tactics" (old style) may do again to the general citizenry. Hence it is fighting Nazi revival tooth and nail.

That has not fazed the Hitlerites. They have vowed to re-

20

build the Nazi Party from Argentina and keep alive the spirit of
Hitler's Naziism. Martin Bormann, Hitler's top aide, has never
been captured. Arrested yes. But never held for trial. It is his
master-plan that has been operating ever since 1945 to organize
a string of undercover Nazi units stretching from Patagonia all
the way back to Germany the Fatherland.

World-wide secret societies are now busy in Germany, operated by Bormann's secret agents. To name a few, there is the
"German Reichs Party", the "Socialist Reichs Party", and the
"Freikorps Deutschland". All these are recently formed political
organizations. The "Freikorps Deutschland" is pledged to over-
throw democracy in Today's Germany. While none of these organizations call themselves "Nazi" -- that word is strictly "taboo"
in Germany -- one simple fact stands out like a sore thumb: The
members are all former Nazis or ardent Nazi supporters.

Anti-semitism (Jew hating) was a basic ingredient of Hitler's
plan in World War II. Unless I am badly mistaken, it is still the
basic ingredient of his followers today.

That is why some 30,000 Jews living in West Germany today
are wondering what the future may hold for them. More than one
incident has occured lately to unnerve them. For example, the
sign of the "swastika" smeared on a synagogue...and upon the
doors the order: "Jews, get out!" has been seen frequently.

In Berlin recently, 25 German students dressed up in the full
regalia of Nazi storm troopers and paraded around Glienicke Park
singing the same old Nazi songs that Hitler inspired.

In Los Angeles, California, on October 25, 1960, an unusual
event took place. Four young "storm troopers" who objected to
the mixed marriage of May Britt to Sammy Davis Jr., decided to
"picket" the theatre in Hollywood where he was appearing. A
half hour before the opening of the Davis show, the four would-be
Nazis tried to put their "picketing plan" into action. They showed
up wearing khaki shirts, black ties, and Nazi swastika armbands.
Each man had a placard proclaiming "Pride in Race and Nation!"

The "plan" was a horrible flop. In fact, it turned out to be
almost fatal for the four determined picketers. Before they could

21

do much picketing, some 100 theatre-goers and passersby took out their anger on the erstwhile "Nazis". The crowd screamed at the four youths, jeered at them and battered them severely about the face and head.

Police rescued the four young men from the crowd's fury, and after hearing their story, sent them home. It seems the defeated "Nazis" had been corresponding with the American Nazi Party in Arlington, Va., where they bought the arm bands for $1.50 each.

The youths explained that they were not "official" members of the Party because they haven't been able to come up with the required dues.

George Lincoln Rockwell is the self-proclaimed "Fuehrer" or leader of the American Nazi Party. He boasts a hard-core of 35 devoted followers at his headquarters in Arlington, Va. Anti-semitism is part of his "mission". It is doubtful that he knows the real Fuehrer is alive. But he continues to pass out the party's anti-Jewish handbills at every public meeting.

All of these undercover organizations serve one purpose... They weaken a nation, a government from within. It is the old Nazi technique of using "ideas" as weapons, namely, the ideas of "hate" and "fear". Back as far as 1920 Hitler had said: "Only by ideologically destroying it from within can Germany conquer Europe. By brute force alone, never!"

Watch out, dear friend, for the "Hate" and "Fear" groups in the cities where you live. These groups are so cleverly disguised with important sounding names, and so efficiently organized, it is often difficult to "smell them out". Watch out, too, for magazines or news publications that hammer out the HATE theme. Here, in plain words, is what they really want of you and me:

"WE WANT YOU to either hate or fear and to ACT from your hate or from your fear! Foment racial violence. Turn brother against brother. Turn your nation into a strife-torn, turmoil-ridden, starving and defenceless humanity. We will take it from there. We shall win. It is just a matter of time!"

★★★★★★★

22

CHAPTER 5

Who Is Mr. Michalek?

◆

The biggest mystery in German UFO circles from 1958 up to the present time, has been : <u>Who is Mr. Michalek?</u> Let me tell you the whole amazing story. I cannot promise to give you the final answer to the riddle -- for I myself do not know that -- but perhaps you can solve the riddle.

I hope so. Because there is apparently much more to the "Michalek Story" than appears on the surface. My job is to uncover as many related facts as possible regarding this highly mysterious personage known as Karl Michalek. I shall leave it up to you to "read between the lines" as the story unfolds.

Firstly, let me say this. Please do not confuse the name of "Michalek" with my own name (Michael X). They sound very much alike, I admit. But Michalek is definitely NOT Michael X (me), and I am definitely not Michalek.

Having settled that, we can go on with the story. It seems that in the year 1958, a mysterious individual by the name of Karl Michalek whose address was Santiago, Chile, South America, began to write some very unusual articles. He sent the unusual writings of his to a newspaper publisher in Germany. The publisher -- whose name was Louis Emrich -- printed everything that Michalek sent to him, and in an unbelievably short time "Michalek" had a large following of readers.

Louis Emrich's newspaper was called: "NEUES EUROPA" or in English, "NEW EUROPE". Until the advent of the articles by Mr. Michalek, the little newspaper presented a variety of different subjects to its readers. Then, all at once, from 1958 onward, the unique Michalek messages began to dominate the publication. The German readers were fascinated, intensely so.

23

The image shows a book cover illustration.

With good reason. Michalek was calmly announcing in the "NEW EUROPE" that he -- Karl Michalek -- was in positive contact with the governmental heads of the planet Venus. The name of the particular intelligent being from Venus who was acting as Michalek's present contact, was "Ase".

Ase and Michalek are desirous, so said the articles, of bringing about everlasting peace and order to our planet Earth. In his series of regularly appearing articles, Karl Michalek presented himself to be a sincere, Godfearing man who believes in the almighty power of the Creator. He is against those world groups who are for promoting war, which Michalek knows will destroy this planet.

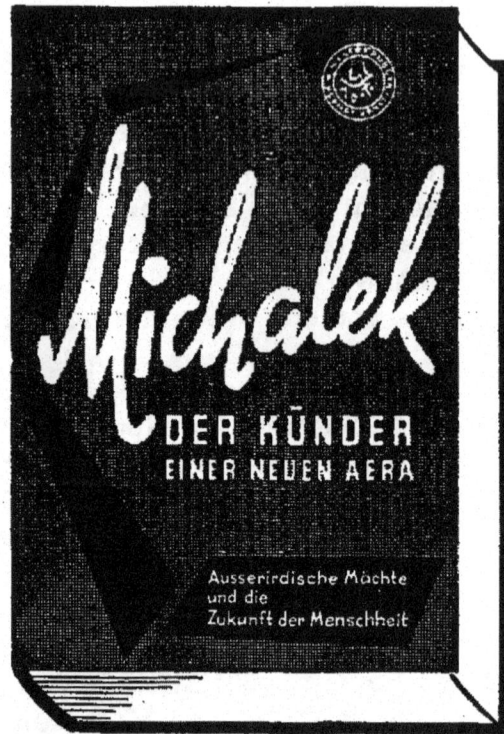

The book which you see pictured at the right, was published in Germany. Its cover says: MICHALEK, The Prophet Of The New Era. Unearthly Forces and the Human Race.

To get the facts about the big "Action-Program" of Michalek, let's turn now to an article which appeared in the "NEW EUROPE in May, 1960: (Translated from the German)

MICHALEK AND HIS WORLD-WIDE ACTION PROGRAM.

"For almost 2000 years we have heard the glad tidings every year: PEACE ON EARTH! Unfortunately this glorious message full of blessings could not be put into realization by the nations because consuming strife was on a rampage everywhere, and a peaceful future was not in sight.

"The different nations -- always on the lookout to expand their countries and their wealth -- were for some time filled with

24

an awful quarrelsome egoism and always ready to swing the war-ax. Now a new, practical way has been found to abolish wars once and forever.

"The spiritual bearer of this great idealistic world idea is Karl Michalek, the President of the coming majestic government of the World Republic of this Earth.

"At the time of the crisis in Berlin at the end of March 1959, Michalek had advised Eisenhower and Khrushchev not to meddle in this conflict by force of weapons at all. If they did meddle in that manner, both Moscow and Washington would be wiped out.

"During the conference in Geneva in May 1959, Michalek sent a telegram to the four ministers in Geneva with the warning they were not to make any decisions which could lead to a third World War. Otherwise, the powers of Venus would see themselves as forced to bring the Earthly leaders to their senses by FORCE. In a note to the two great powers Michalek had explicitly demanded in July 1959 that all experiments with atom bombs should cease immediately.

"ULTIMATUM TO KRUSHCHEV: On March 12, 1960 Michalek put the Ultimatum to Khrushchev to withdraw the Russian weapons for mass destruction which were directed to other countries..... Otherwise he (Mr. K.) as well as all the members of his government would have to reckon with the most severe measures of punishment. (Namely, and invasion by the Venus fleet. M.X.)

"From this, one can see that Michalek is actively interceding in a confused, unsafe, abysmal world politic and wants to bring about an absolute peaceful handling of world politics. He alone could never have accomplished this. Who has been standing by him, and who has strengthened his backbone? The chief leadership of the planet Venus, who has the fullest confidence in him, has done this!

"He (Michalek) has been chosen by them to become the President of the coming nation-uniting World Republic of this Earth. He has also had several contacts and personal discussions with the leader of the proposed landing action, the Commander in Chief of the 3rd Venusian Space Fleet...Ase.

25

"With the announced New Order which is going to be established on this Earth, a new, more hopeful Age will begin in the world history...with the help and active support of the powers from Venus. Among other things it will bring the following important changes:

(1) Through the reorganization of the four continents --Europe, Africa, America, Asia -- all of the present existing States and nations will be declared Provinces. No boundaries will separate the States or countries, dividing the nations. There will only be Provincial boundaries.

(2) The earthly world republic will consist of 72 World-Provinces in the future.

(3) In all of the 72 World-Provinces capital punishment will be introduced for crimes like murder, robbery, arson, narcotics.

(4) Within the new earthly community of the nations a truly economical system will be established. The welfare of the entire humanity will depend upon the frictionless functioning of this economic system. All earthly nations shall be justly dealt with, and the world-wide hunger catastrophes which have become so permanent up to now, shall be abolished entirely.

(5) The whole system of finance will be put on an entirely new basis. A new monetary medium will be issued by the majestic government of the World Republic, which will have the same unified value in all the countries (Provinces) of this Earth.

(6) Nothing can be bought or paid for with the standard money which is being used now, after the Day of the Landing. On that Day the change to the new unit-money will be made.

(7) The existence of all colonial possessions will come to an end with the Day of the Landing.

(8) All military agencies and authorities will necessarily be dissolved in all the ex-States and world provinces within 30 days after the proclamation of the World Republic. Furthermore it is to be said: the people of the planet Venus do not want to conquer or exploit our Earth as our present earthly men of state would do

26

in a reverse case. But they are coming to save humanity of this Earth from atomic destruction which is inevitable should World War III come.

"FLYING SAUCERS have been sighted in more than a thousand cases, which sightings have been officially registered. Quite often they have landed on this Earth secretly and unobserved. A certain proof of this, is the fact that EXPERTS FROM VENUS have been living here on this Earth for the last 15 years. They speak English and German. (Note this. M.X.)

MICHALEK PREDICTS THE VENUS UFO LANDING!

At the beginning of his "career" Michalek -- for some strange reason -- decided to announce publicly in the "NEW EUROPE" publication, that "Der Tag X" (X-Day) was about to happen. A Landing of Venus Space ships would take place, said Michalek confidently, in the earth year 1958... on X-Day.

You can, I am sure, imagine the great excitement this bold prediction caused among Michalek's followers. In thrilled anticipation, everybody awaited "Der Tag X". On X-Day in December 1958, a whole fleet of Venus Space Ships would land in the city of Berlin, Germany, for all eyes to behold in awesome wonder.

December came...and went. No fleet from Venus showed up. In fact, to the bitter disappointment of readers of the "NEW EUROPE", there was not a single UFO anywhere to be seen.

What had happened? No one had the slightest notion, until Michalek explained. The chief leader of the people of the planet Venus -- said Michalek -- had passed away unexpectedly on December 17, 1958. The Venusian President, whose name was "Urun", had suddenly died at the age of 193. Ase, the Commander of the Third Space Fleet, saw himself forced to delay the landing maneuver for a short period of time.

Two years later, Michalek again predicted "Der Tag X". This time, he stated, it was fixed and irrevocable. The date of the Venus Fleet landing was to be April 21, 1960! (Note how X-Day was set for one day after Hitler's birth month and day, April 20th)

27

April 21st arrived...<u>uneventfully.</u> Again for some unknown
reason the Venusian UFO fleet had seen fit to stay away. This
time, the failure of the Spaceships to "arrive" as Michalek had
promised, brought forth a storm of protesting letters from readers
of the "NEW EUROPE". The chart below shows the curve of Michalek's success and popularity from 1958 to May, 1960. It is based on the great number of letters from the public which have been
sent to the Editor of the "NEW EUROPE" newspaper.

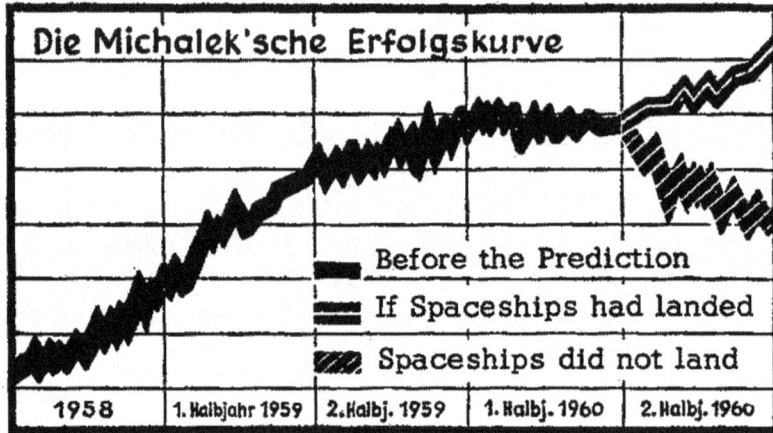

Die Michalek'sche Erfolgskurve

Before the Prediction
If Spaceships had landed
Spaceships did not land

| 1958 | 1. Halbjahr 1959 | 2. Halbj. 1959 | 1. Halbj. 1960 | 2. Halbj. 1960 |

Notice how -- from 1958 to 1959 --Michalek's following increased by leaps and bounds in all parts of the world. Member-
ship in his organization -- The Supreme World Republic -- grew
rapidly from a few hundred members to more than 30,000. From
the beginning of 1959 to April 21,1960, the curve of favor of Michalek's popularity went way up. But since April 21, 1960, a
noticeable decline toward the negative side has been observed,

Because the predicted Venus Landing didn't take place --and
hasn't to the date of this writing -- the curve of Michalek's success has sunk into the negative realm, and Michalek has sunk
with it. INTERPOL in Austria takes a very dim view of his claims
and is opposed to him. Even Michalek's former staunch supporters, including the disillusioned Louis Emrich, have fallen away.

It is true that Karl Michalek's broken promises have left a
great many disillusioned and disappointed people, as the natural
aftermath of what many good Germans feel was a great fraud . In
your considered opinion, is Michalek just a naive "world reform-
er", a "harmless dreamer" or a real swindler in the grand style?

★★★★★★★

28

Chapter 6

"For some time, now, I have been the one designated to be President of the highest governmental authority of the coming World Republic. I have been so designated by the power of the Chief Leader of the planet Venus..."

The above words were the sentiments of Karl Michalek as he announced them to the world in a published message in 1959. If we look back a few short years in history to the year 1945, we discover a most significant fact:

Adolph Hitler was drawing up his "last will and testament". It was, in reality, his political will or party blueprint.

It appointed the next or forthcoming German Government. In this will, Hitler did not name a second Fuehrer to succeed him. He named Admiral Karl Doenitz as the next President of the Reich. Goebbels was named for the post of Reich Chancellor, and Martin Bormann was named the Party Minister.

Note this. The real power head of the Reich government is the Reich Chancellor. (Hitler's title). Joseph Goebbels was named Chancellor, but he was eliminated by the Nazis at the end of the war, then the present true boss of the new Reich would be none other than...yes, you guessed it...Hitler himself.

The President, though, would be Admiral Karl Doenitz. It is possible that Karl Michalek is in actuality the illegitimate son of Adolph Hitler and that his authority comes -- not from the Leader of the planet Venus -- but from Adolph Hitler and the Nazi Party. At any rate, INTERPOL is keeping a close watch on him.

Mind you, I say it is "possible". I do not claim it is the gospel truth or a proven certainty. No. It's a simple hypothesis and nothing more. So far Michalek has not "delivered the goods" in regard to his predictions of UFO landings, and his own broken promises have dubbed him a charlatan, a hoaxer on the grand scale. Those who formerly believed in him, now DO NOT.

My point is this. Is Michalek working with Hitler? If so, he is not kidding about the existence of UFO's. The Hitler group would have -- if my theory is correct -- a goodly number of bell-shaped, hat-shaped, and oval-shaped UFO's built by now.

Louis Emrich, whose personal faith in Michalek must have been badly shaken when Venus ships didn't land, had written:

Alleged picture of Hitler in disguise and wearing
civilian clothing after was rumored to escape to
South America.

"As has been explicitly assured by the authoritative side,
there is not the slightest doubt about the reality of the Proclamation Program of Michalek's. The difficulties which have come
up are mainly the fault of the inner organization. Several of the
new members of Michalek's chief staff do not qualify to the re-
quirements to the extent that had been expected of them. Furthermore, inner and outer political difficulties have come up which
had not been calculated with..." (from the "NEW EUROPE")

WHO, I wonder, is "the authoritative side"? Might it be --
as we suspect -- the Nazi Party? Or is it Venus? May I submit
that if it were really Venus as Michalek is claiming, there would
be no such thing as "delays" in the landings. Any Space Fleet
with a thousand or more years of experience in space flight would
have no problem landing "on time" if they wanted to.

No, it is much more likely that Hitler has been hiding his
UFO secret all along, since 1940 perhaps. It is quite conceivable
that the Nazi High Command is still interested in world rulership,
and expects to use the UFO's to enable it to achieve just that.
The fifteen years since war's end is a long time. It is certainly
a long enough duration of time to make many new plans.

The Michalek story may be a part of their plans...a prelimin-
ary test phase that for some reason, perhaps a good reason, had
to be discontinued. If our hypothesis is right, Hitler has the
UFO secret. And if we could manage to look in on his Argentine
Hideout , we'd no doubt see quite an armada of earth-built UFO's.
Not only that. It is also likely we'd find the craft well-armed.

30

But not with conventional weapons. No, we'd probably find the Hitler UFO's armed with ultra high-frequency electromagnetic beam devices capable of stalling any ordinary electrical system such as the ignition system of cars, trucks, planes, etc.

If those earth-made Nazi UFO's are built of secret metal alloys, they'd probably have to "import" certain metals from some other country. Logical one would be Brazil. It's right next door, and it's fabulously rich in metals such as tin, zinc, etc. This could account for the exceedingly high number of UFO sightings in Brazil. Those UFO's could be quietly transporting the needed metals out of Brazilian mines into the Patagonia stronghold.

Photo courtesy of Max. B. Miller.

In 1958 the above photograph was taken of a genuine UFO as it flew over Trinidad Island, which is just off Brazil. It was seen by the men aboard a navy survey ship who were taking part in IGY program explorations at the time. This may indeed be a Nazi UFO.

31

To the Brazilians and Argentinans, the sighting of UFO's is getting too commonplace to even comment on it anymore. During a recent 14 month period, no less than 149 sightings were officially reported in Brazil. Whole communities of hundreds of people sighted the objects at the same time!

Why were these UFO's often seen glowing bright red, orange, etc? Use of an "electrified system" for motive power. That produces an electromagnetic "forcefield" around the craft. Vikton schauberger, you will recall, invented such an engine in 1940. Electromagnetism creates a force-field in which certain energies developed in the process can begin to "incandesce" or glow.

In 1957 the saga of the "Flying Egg" began. On November 2 and 3 of that year, people in Levelland, western Texas, reported seeing a UFO shaped like an egg. It was about 200 feet long, and glowed brightly as though it was on fire. Most of the observers stated it was about 200 feet in the air when they saw it. The force-field of the UFO stalled motor cars on the highway.

On Nov. 5, Mr. J. Wolfe, a citizen of San Raphael, California, sighted the huge glowing oval-shaped UFO. It was sighted also by at least one woman resident of San Raphael. On the same day, the Coast Guard Cutter "Sebago" sighted a UFO resembling a "brilliant planet" moving at tremendous speed over the Gulf of Mexico.

On Nov. 5, Mr. Rheinhold Schmidt of Kearney, Nebraska, reported that he had "contacted" a strange, oval-shaped UFO near Kearney. Schmidt said his car engine went dead. He got out to see what was wrong and there was the UFO close by on the ground. He was invited inside the craft, and there met four men and one woman. They all spoke "English and High German". They told Schmidt they were from the planet Saturn.

On Nov. 9, at Weatherly High School in Lansford, Pa., the "Flying Egg" was seen in the sky by eight Junior High students who happened to be outside at the time. According to the children, the "oval-shaped thing" came down about as high as the rooftops. It rotated at a high speed, causing the four red lights on its rim to appear blurred. The students made a detailed sketch of it. We have reproduced the sketch for you on the next page.

32

On August 15, 1960 -- three years later -- the "flying Egg" was back again. This time it showed up at Red Bluff, California. The San Francisco Chronicle carried this bold headline : STATE COPS RACE 'FLYING SAUCER'. In reality, the strange object was NOT shaped like a 'saucer' at all. It was OVAL-SHAPED, just as the UFO was that had been seen in 1957. It looked the same and performed the same way.

Briefly, here is what the SF newspaper said : "Red object sighted by Patrolmen. RED BLUFF, Aug. 15, 1960. A mysterious Flying Thing giving off a red glow has been sighted over the cattle country 18 miles south of here. It was as big as an airliner (about 100-200 ft in length) and shaped like a football. (oval) Sometimes it just hung silently in the air only 200 feet off the ground. (the UFO seen at Levelland, Texas acted the same way.)

If this "Flying Egg" UFO we have just been talking about is not "made on Mars", that is, if it isn't interplanetary --although we realize some UFO's do come from "outside" our planet --then what? Then perhaps it and a few other UFO's like it, was born right here on Earth, in the shelter of vast Patagonia!

C. Wright Mills, noted author of "The Power Elite", and more recently, "Listen, Yankee!", in writing briefly of Argentina said: "...armed men are in the pampas". I ask, "What are they doing there? Why isn't that fertile land being used for cattle and for ranchland as it ought to be? You and I don't need three guesses. Follow me closely. Is it not strange indeed that our man of mystery -- Michalek -- had released the following information :

33

TRILOGY OF THE UNKNOWN
"The scientists of Venus
have learned to overcome completely the so-called law of
gravitation. A certain proof of
of UFO landings is the fact
that experts from Venus have
been living here on this Earth
for the last 15 years. THEY
SPEAK ENGLISH AND GERMAN."

It is conceivable that Michalek is actually thinking of the
Nazi UFO scientists of Patagonia, instead of true Venus people. It
has been 15 years since the Nazis lost the war. Well-educated
Nazis can speak in English, switch to German and then to Spanish!

Vice Adm. R.H.Hillenkoetter (Ret.) -- a former director of
the CIA in America -- recently said that "behind the scenes, high-
ranking Air Force officers are soberly concerned about the UFO's."
Why? Does the Air Force expect an "attack" or invasion of the
Earth by UFO's from another planet? I don't think so. General
Nathan Twining of the U.S. Air Force (Ret.) commented in 1954: "If
they come from Mars and there is a world and a civilization that
far ahead of us, I don't think we have anything to worry about."

I agree. But earth-built UFO's are a different matter entirely. What do you think would happen if a whole fleet of UFO's manned by earthlings from a secret place on Earth were to actually
make a landing in Berlin? Or in Washington, D.C.? What if they
-- the pilots of the earth-built UFO's -- made use of "electromagnetic" devices to cause all electrical power systems in those big
cities to suddenly go completely, utterly DEAD?

Imagine it. All electrical systems in the cities "stalled" by
the UFO devices. No electricity for lights, communications, or for
anything else we usually power with electricity. Our military
couldn't even send up its Nike guided missiles to intercept the
UFO's, since they are fired electrically! Then a voice is heard in
the air: Your city, your nation is helpless. We are here to bring
a new way of life to this world. We ask you not to fear us but to
follow these instructions at once....!"

You take it from there. But don't panic. So far it is only
imaginary, and God willing it will never happen. We are not talking about an interplanetary invasion, but an earthly blitz by the
earthly UFO's. The real reason, perhaps, why the Air Force is "soberly concerned about the UFO's" right now.

- 34 -

Chapter 7

EVENTS HAPPENING on Earth, in the Earth and above Earth at this very moment certainly bear close watching. None of us would like to be caught short, or with his head in the sand like the ostrich.

ARGENTINA in particular, deserves our special attention from now on. The Nazi influence is active there, far more so than we Americans realize. And we have not seen the last of their UFO's.

Those earth-built UFO's are fabulous inventions. They can be turned into the greatest weapon mankind has ever seen...or they can be the true means of earthman's liberation from planetary bondage. Will those who have this secret -- and in this book we have reasoned that a hidden power in Argentina does have it -- will they use it to plunge us all into a third World War?

If we mean war as we've been accustomed to think of it, the answer is a positive no. Why not? Because war, under the 20th century conditions (atom bombs, super-gas warfare, biological and radiological warfare, etc. is now a self-defeating enterprise. All-out war is ridiculous now and everybody knows it.

However, the subtle -- "nibble warfare" -- is not only quite possible but workable. It is the artful technique of "nibbling" a chunk of somebody else's territory little by little, so it won't be noticed. It's a quiet invasion of a country by steady nibblers who pretty soon have moved in completely and taken things over. But it's so quiet and protracted you hardly know it's happening.

The real battle today is for the minds and souls of men, and the stakes are big -- all the earth and all the people on it. The fight itself revolves around one main issue. Will you and I keep our God-given right of "Individualism", with all the liberty and freedom that implies, or...will we sell-out our heritage for some illusory mess of pottage we'd get if we turn over all power to a totalitarian government or dictator? Who, among men, knows how to run your life for you with true wisdom from cradle to grave?

The simple object is this: to unite mankind everywhere in the spirit of true brotherly love, understanding and peace. To allow all men to be of active assistance and help to the total humanity on earth and elsewhere. To unite all human beings in a mighty, purposeful, indivisible body that will "outlaw" all that is detrimental to true progress of body, mind and soul.

FREE ENERGY, if released to this planet, could change things on earth as they have never been changed before. It could -- undoubtedly -- usher in a New Order of The Ages. Imagine it. a constant supply of free electric energy taken right from the atmos-

- 35 -

phere by everybody. Yes, a universal power such as Free-Energy could release man from many of the burdens now present in our world money systems. But who has such a secret?

The Nazis! If they have the original Vikton Schauberger "Electro-Magnetic" engine -- or improved versions of it -- they have Free-Energy. The UFO engine runs on power taken directly from the atmosphere. And that is quite inexhaustible.

I talked recently with a brilliant man from Europe. Holland, I believe, is his native land. It is, however, no effort for him to speak seven different languages fluently...including German. I asked him if he could give me any pertinent facts about the Nazis' use of Free-Energy, since I knew he had access to certain "inside information."

"Yes," my friend replied, "it is known that the Nazis have a Free-Energy motor, and used it in 1958 to propel a U-boat between Europe and Buenos Aires. It is also believed by many of us that there is an underwater station -- built by the Nazis -- somewhere in the Atlantic Ocean between Germany and Argentina. A stopover place, no doubt, for Nazi subs and UFO's."

I thought to myself, amazing..simply amazing. I inquired,

"Just where are the Nazis, right now?"

- 36 -

"Everywhere. In all countries. Not only Patagonia, but the United States, Canada, Africa...and even in far-off Antarctica. The Nazi can never be content nor satisfied to just stop what he is working on. He must go ahead and achieve it. You must realize that the Nazi believes he is working for a New Age...the coming World Government that will benefit everyone."

I could understand that, even agree with it. What I forever refuse to go along with is the use of force and brutality and killings. Naturally, I had to ask him the big question.

"Do you think they will use the same old "storm trooper" methods -- violence, strongarm tactics, mass bloodshed -- to bring in their idea of a New Era in which man will be given the scientific keys to free energy, true space travel, and so forth?"

The Hollander smiled . "Negative minds might look at it that way, " he answered, "But we could take another viewpoint. We could imagine that the Nazis have learned, through past experience, that there is a limit -- a definite limit -- to the use of force destructively. Beyond a certain point, negative use of force has no value and becomes self-defeating to the user. They may have found, in passing far beyond the limits of orthodox science -- that all humanity is ONE, and must move upward together.

"It is my feeling," he said, "that within possibly the next five years, the Nazi leaders will suddenly return to the world scene and say : 'You have forgotten us but we are still here. We realize now that some thing we did in the past were wrong, and we are willing to make up for them. Our scientific secrets can open up new doors of UNLIMITED PROGRESS for all mankind. Here is what we have to offer all the people of the whole world...!"

Our discussion came to a close, and my learned friend departed. Alone again, I opened my Bible to Chapters 11 & 12 in the Book of Daniel. I'm glad I did. It clarified many world events, some have already happened and some which are due to happen. I urge you to read it too. Like Nostradamus, Daniel "saw true".

At this point I'm sensing your thought. "The Nazis -- will they return to our world scene in brilliantly glowing UFO's?" Our old friend, Michael Nostradamus, thought so. He wrote:

37

TRILOGY OF THE UNKNOWN

(1) They shall think to have seen the
        sun in the night,
(2) When the hog half a man shall be
        seen.
(3) Noise, singing, battles in the sky
        shall be perceived,
(4) And brute beasts shall be heard
        to speak.

The first line (1): refers to the brightly glowing or sun-like appearance of the Nazi UFO's when seen in the night sky.

The second line (2): could be naming Martin Bormann. A boar is also a "hog". Boar sounds the same as "Bor". Half of the concealed name is "man" or "mann". Result: Bormann. !

The third line (3): means that the Nazi UFO's will be challenged in the sky, no doubt by our national defense system if it is operable . Possibly outer space craft will play a part also.

The fourth line (4): I leave to you, dear reader, to interpret in your own way. Don't skip over it lightly. It's important. Yes my friend, you must use your own "6th Sense" as regards whom you will trust, and whom you will serve now and in the days ahead. I'll be at your side to help, if you need me. So will the Christ-minded beings of Venus and other planets. They too are saying "WE WANT YOU!" but only to guide and set you free.

We desire FREEDOM, not slavery. Because you and I have a vision, my friend. A vision that is real. We see Man of Earth coming into his true heritage of DIVINE LIBERTY wherein human beings transcend both hate and fear. This true approach to life may well be called the "RULE OF LOVE" on planet Earth. Love (higher spiritual appreciation) stands as the great "Balancer" between Brute Force on one side and Cold Intellect on the other. It is the Christ way. Every man shall one day walk this way.

Those who do not join a "hate" or a "fear" group may be in the minority -- increasingly so as time goes by. But if their Love, Courage and Wisdom is great they will have the HELP OF HEAVEN. This is my faith. And I believe it is also yours. It is up to us awaken this higher LOVE in the hearts of our brothers.

38

TRILOGY OF THE UNKNOWN

Our world, my friend, needs love. Not the sickly, soft brand of sentimental weakness, but deep understanding love. That's where you come in. Because if you're anything like me and the rest of my New Age friends, you don't believe in weakness.

Brutality, bloodshed and horror is not your "cup of tea" either. Like me, you are in search of a better way. Then just what is it that can stand up to the old, unnatural, inhumane "RULE OF FOR-CE" in our world? TRUTH. It alone can set us all free.

And the truth is that the "RULE OF LOVE" must begin to exert its divine sway in the present-day world right now or we may see this world transformed into another bloody bath again. This must not be. . . and you and I can do our part to prevent it.

A very wise man once asked me, "Michael, how many sides are there to a coin?"

I looked at the fifty-cent piece he was holding in his hand as he spoke. I replied that I saw two sides.

"Wrong," he said, "Besides the 'heads' side and the 'tails' side, there is a third side...the edge of the coin!"

Fascinated, I listened while he explained. "Few people are aware that there is a third side to every coin. Fewer still know that the third side is greater in a sense than either of the other two sides. Each of the two sides is bounded by the edge, is it not? In other words, the size or diameter of each side is LIMIT-ED. It cannot go beyond that limit, right?"

"Right, " I answered. Then he smiled.

"The third side which is the edge of the coin, is NOT BOUND-ED by anything, it's unlimited. You could roll the coin on its edge forever (theoretically) and it would keep on going into in-finity. The same thing is also true of Love!"

I never forgot that symbolic lesson. The Truth that you and I and a glorious legion of other awakened souls on earth and be-yond it, have found the mystic "Third Side" of the coin. It is the "Christ-Love" within our hearts that shall redeem all of us.

✦✦✦✦✦✦✦✦✦✦

39

Michael X Investigates
The Reality of the Serpent Race
Inside the Earth
by Timothy Green Beckley

If you think David Icke invented the premise that there is a serpent race existing amongst us humans on Earth,better ask Michael X if he can add anything to this concept.

Reptilian creatures have been around as long as humankind. Of course Lilith tempted Adam in the Garden of Eden with a serpent and hey we wish sometimes she would have done a better job as a seductress so we could see more of those lovely ladies in the buff without having to spend money on Playboy or internet porn.

If you go back as far as the mid 1940s, a "science fiction" author by the name of Richard S. Shaver seems to have let the cat out of the bag, when he wrote about his adventures with all kinds of weird underground dwellers. Among the species, he claims to have encountered include seven feet tall reptilians and serpents who reside, Shaver insisted, in a vast cavern world most of us know absolutely nothing about. From time to time, these serpents drag or kidnap humans to their underground lairs to torture and even eat them. It's a messy situation that most turned their backs on. Shaver heard voices in his head. A lot of people just tried to tune them out!

What developed into "The Shaver Mystery" attracted a large faithful following who waited anxiously each month for copies of *Amazing Stories* to hit the newsstands. This simple pulp magazine, with its scantly clad cover girls being mauled by denizens of the deep space or deep earthly region, had a dedicated audience thanks to its highly creative editor. Ray A. Palmer was a young man out of Chicago who was always looking for something different to spark his reader's imagination and to increase circulation. One day an unsolicited manuscript arrived in the mail and he knew he had the "next best thing." Richard Shaver's original manuscript titled *I Remember Lemuria* had been tossed aside by the publication's assistant editor Robert Brown, but RAP retrieved it from the circular file. Sure the script needed some editing but all the elements of Jules Verne and H. P. Lovecraft were there. The adventure of exploring the caves, the horrible creatures with bulging eyes. Palmer printed the story and the rest is history. Over ten thousand readers claimed to have had similar experiences. They had heard the voices Shaver was tormented by, encountered scaly reptilians and had even visited their underground chambers deep within the bowels of the earth which were more like S and M dungeons than anything else (Shaver claimed he could hear people being whipped and otherwise tortured).

Yes! They had been inside the caves, and those who had been lucky enough not to be made into human stew, came back with all manner of terrifying tales.

According to Richard Shaver, Ray Palmer and other writers, there remains a vast world beneath our feet that we know almost nothing about, although such accounts are part of the legends and lore of many races. Some of the stories about this cavern zone have filtered back to the surface but are not easily confirmed. Yes! There are those who have been kidnapped and kept captive in some vast tunnel system all over the world. Yes! There are various openings, but all well concealed. The two largest openings can be found at the North and South Poles where vessels have been known to disappear mysteriously. Explorers also tell many weird tales of phantom flying ships to saucer-shaped discs observed near these supposed polar openings. Their stories have fueled the imagination of many, including Admiral Richard Byrd who is said to have actually lead an expedition into the poles where he encountered giants over eight feet tall – the local inhabitants – as well as a contingent of Nazis who left for "higher ground" toward the close of WWII. Here they reside in their own settlements and fly one of the flying saucers they created with the assistance of mediums who were able to contact other dimensional beings who know how to get around in space much easier than Uncle Sam.

Here is Michael X's report *Rainbow City and the Inner Earth People* followed up by a rare reprint of the Heffelin manuscript which has not been in print since the early 1950s and which Michael X and others make reference to in their works.

So hang onto your hat and be prepared to hear what was not intended to be spoken about except in selective circles, but for which we must thank our dear whistle blower friend Michael X who managed to release this important conspiratorial information —before he mysteriously vanished from the scene never to be heard from again.

.

Rainbow City
and
Inner Earth People
by Michael X

TRILOGY OF THE UNKNOWN
RAINBOW CITY AND INNER EARTH PEOPLE

- by -

MICHAEL X

* * *

This is an Educational and Inspirational Course of Study, especially written and intended for NEW AGE individuals everywhere. The following SEVEN chapters are contained herein:

1. "SAUCERS FROM INNER EARTH"

2. "A STRANGE GREAT VALLEY"

3. "THE RAINBOW CITY PEOPLE"

4. "COLONEL FAWCETT'S FATE"

5. "THE SUN-GOD'S SECRET"

6. "REASON FOR HUSH-HUSH"

7. "WHAT DO THEY WANT?"

* * *

Statements in this Course are based on Scientific and Scriptural Findings. No claim is made as to what the information cited may do in any given case and the Publishers assume no obligation for opinions expressed or implied herein by the author.

Dear New Age Student:

Stand by for Adventure...gigantic
adventure!

Come with me now, far beyond the
South Pole...into the center of the
Great Unknown. Our destination: A
Strange Great Valley. We shall now
travel together to the same valley
that Admiral Richard E. Byrd reportedly discovered in the year 1947.

What is our purpose--our big objective? To unravel several mysteries.
One: Are the UFO's -- flying saucers
or spaceships -- in our skies coming
from INSIDE the earth instead of from
other planets? Might they be coming
from BOTH places? Why?

Two: Does the fabled "Rainbow City"
exist somewhere in Antarctica? If so,
where? Who lives there? Do they use
flying discs and come from the earth's
interior? What kind of people might
we expect to find inside the earth?

Stupendous MYSTERIES? Yes, but that
is why you and I are traveling the
HIGH Road together... This may prove
to be our greatest exploring mission.

Oh yes, one more thing. We are going
to turn our mental searchlight inside
this Earth we live upon. I caution
you to "expect the unexpected" because
ANYTHING could happen. But don't let
yourself get too excited. I'm counting
on you to be a "clearthinking, quick-
acting companion" on this BIG EXPEDITION.

                    Your Friend,

                    MICHAEL X

Chapter 1

Are some of the Flying Saucers coming from INSIDE the earth? A few years ago this question would have seemed ridiculous. Now it doesn't.

Raymond Palmer, Editor of a wonderful little magazine entitled FLYING SAUCERS, recently published a most important article on this subject. It was titled: SAUCERS FROM EARTH! In his article, Ray brought forth an astonishing amount of evidence for the idea that perhaps our earth is not solid, but hollow. You know how a doughnut has a hole through its center. The earth also, surmises Ray Palmer, may look like that...like a "doughnut". Rather than being spherical as we've always thought, maybe this old planet is "doughnut shaped"...with mysterious parts to it on the "inner side" that we simply don't know about.

If so, and a wealth of evidence now begins to shout in quite a loud voice that it IS so, many of those "unidentified flying objects" we call Flying Saucers may indeed be coming from some place inside this very earth. A place previously unsuspected by most of us because of two things. One, the difficulty of getting there. Two, science on earth hasn't given us any reason to believe such a place exists.

Fortunately for us deeper students of life, there is one other source of information we can turn to. It's known as "Occult Science" which simply means "hidden" science. It is a great body of knowledge commonly unknown to most people. But, as you probably realize, that "secret knowledge" derived from the teachings of ancient races, really isn't the least bit "secret" to those of us who like to explore.

One very unusual "hidden teaching" of the ancients pertained to the Inner Earth. According to Doreal, who is the highly respected founder of the Brotherhood of The White Temple in Sedalia, Colorado, ancient teachings have it that the earth is hollow and inhabited. In Doreal's book, "THE INNER EARTH", he describes the inner earth according to ancient wisdom teachings. The ancients say that only the out-

- 3 -

er crust of the earth is subject to heat, from a layer of hot
lava near the surface. Volcanoes are due to that hot layer.

But go down into the earth 150 miles and what happens?
No more uncomfortable heat. Now it's quite comfortable in
temperature, and we see a vast system of caverns and tunnels.
It is said that a series of great caves and channels is to be
found inside the earth just below that belt of hot lava. One
of those channels completely encircles the earth inside, so
that you could ride all around the inside of the world through
that channel and come back to the point you started from.

Going deeper below those caves and channels, you'd come
to some colossal room caverns. Some so big, Doreal states,
that a whole city could be lost within its huge spaces! But
down farther than those big rooms is the fascinating part. We
now enter the deepest "Inner Circle" of the earth. Here is a
tremendous hollow space and in the exact center of that hollow
space -- floating freely -- you would see what looks like a
small version of our sun. It's the central globe or "sun"
inside the earth and of course it energizes the "Inner Earth".

Wonderful! But let's do a little comparing. How about
our own modern, up-to-the-minute conclusions of the scientists?
For instance, what facts about our earth's inner structure were
learned by geologists in 1958 during the IGY explorations?

From a world wide study of earthquake waves, it was found
that this earth consists of a number of layers. The outermost
crust goes down about 250 miles. Below this is a thick layer
called the "mantle". It consists of four different layers, actually, and penetrates downward to 1800 miles. Next comes the
"outer core", the "transition layer" and the "inner core".

On page 5 are diagrams you'll find very interesting. A
total of four different drawings are shown, each one providing
us with vital information about the structure of earth. Note
that while there are some discrepancies in measurements, among
the ancient and modern findings, still there is agreement on a
great many points. Modern findings show an area inside the
earth which they term the "outer core". It is thought to be a
liquid layer. The ancients say it contains air and that air
acts like a fluid under certain tests. The "inner core" could
very well be the small "central sun" within the earth.

Admiral Richard E. Byrd discovered a mysterious land beyond the South Pole during his 1947 Exploration. He called it
"the center of the great unknown, and the most important discovery of all time." What did Byrd mean by that statement?
Was he telling us.."I have found a Great Doorway leading into
the interior of the earth. A whole new world exists there!"

- 4 -

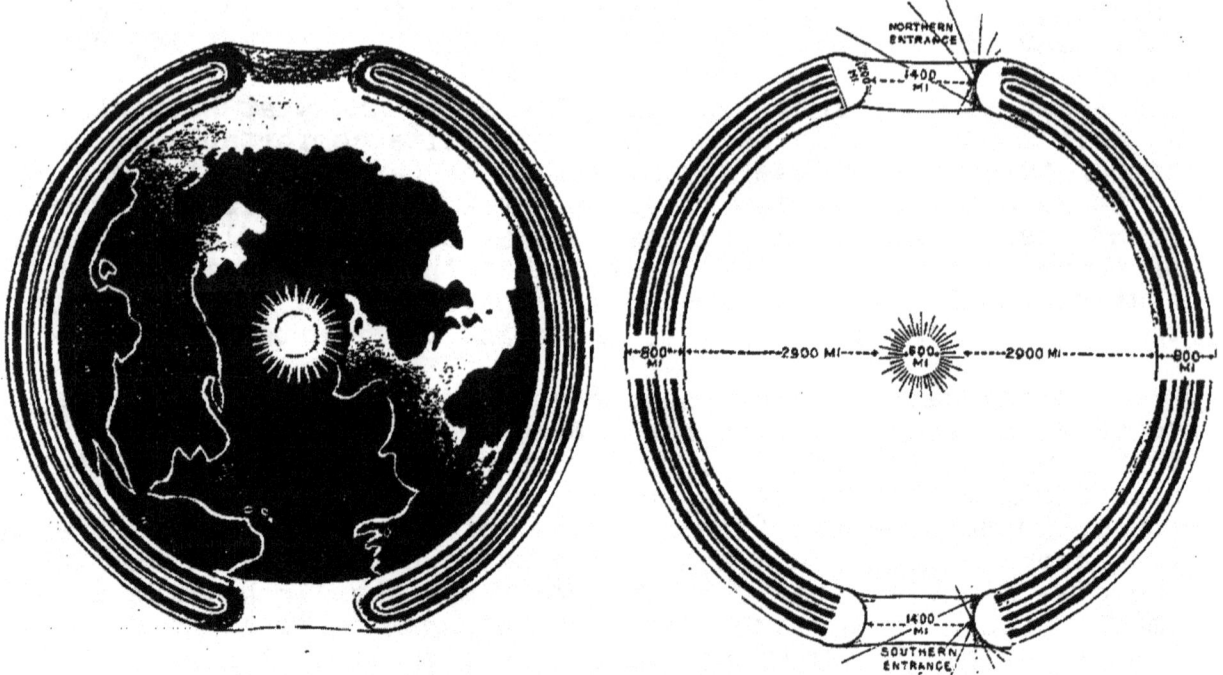

1 & 2.   The two diagrams above appeared
         in a book titled: "A Journey To
The Earth's Interior".   It was published
in 1929 by Marshall B. Gardner. Diagrams
show the earth as a hollow sphere with
polar openings and a small central sun.

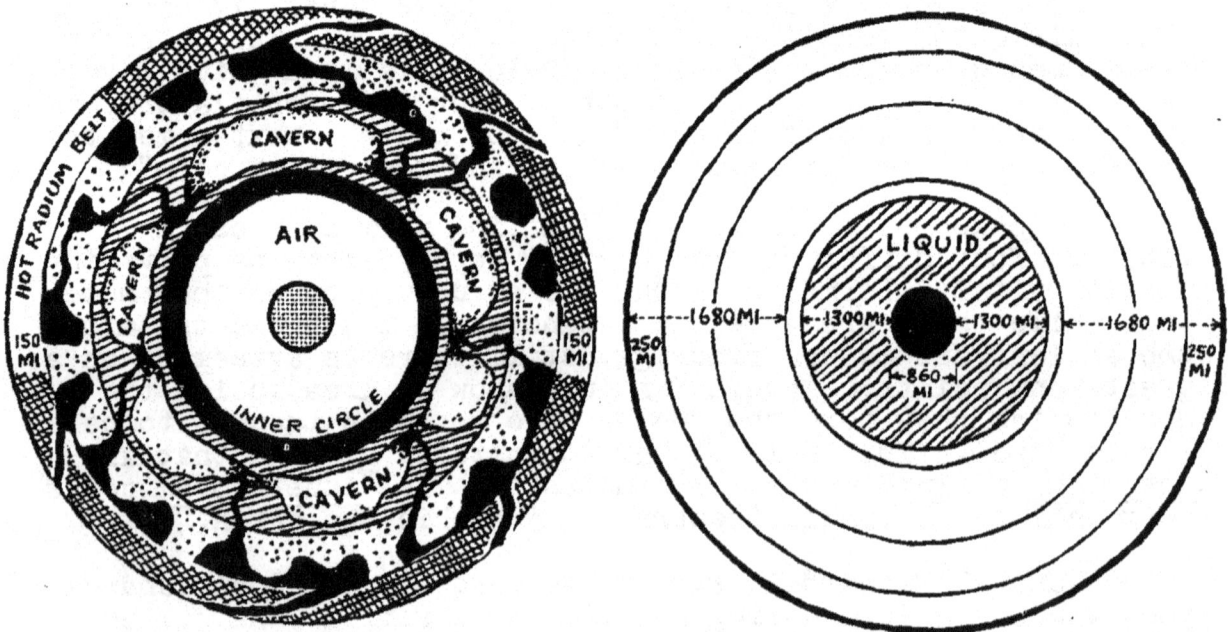

3. Ancient Teachings claim that
    a great "Cavern World" exists.

4. 1958 findings of modern
    IGY scientist explorers.

- 5 -

TRILOGY OF THE UNKNOWN

In January 1955, at a four day conference of the Theosophical Society in Rio de Janeiro, another voice spoke out for the very same theory. It was not the voice of a wild-eyed dreamer. It was the sober opinion of Brazilian Navy Commander Justino Strauss, a practical, hard-headed realist.

"One should not ignore the legends of enchanted cities, said Justino, "I believe these mysterious engines (saucers) come from the center of the earth, where it has long been believed that life exists to a degree far advanced over our own civilization."

Strauss felt that the disappearance of Col. Percy H. Fawcett, who vanished in the Amazon jungles years ago (in 1925) while searching for a rumored City of Wealth, was connected with the operations of the people who dwell in the hollow center of the earth.

At first thought it may seem fantastic...utterly fantastic, to suppose even for a moment that the earth is hollow. But what are the facts? Isn't almost every functional object in nature, like a bone or a living cell or a skull or an atom, hollow to a surprising extent? An atom, for example, has a central nucleus or proton at its center. Around that center any given number of electrons may revolve. But between those electrons and the nucleus is hollow space.

Flying Saucers from inside our earth? Why not? If we conclude that our planet is also a "functional" object, designed by an unlimited Creative Intelligence to "house" vast numbers of living beings...an amazing thought hits us. The Earth Realm may have more living quarters than we have imagined. If it doesn't, we could possibly run into a major problem in overpopulation at the rate we are going.

I think the Earth Realm is comprised of (1) Region of earth's surface, (2) Region of outer space above the earth, (3) Region of inner space inside the earth.

If all three of these Regions are habitable, if human beings can possibly dwell on, above or within this planet, I can assure you they are living there right now. Poeple are certainly living ON the earth. There is no question about that. Do people live above the earth? Yes, say the Space Contactees. Outer space people live in the spacial regions above and beyond our planet. These are not the people who dwell on other planets such as Venus, Mars, etc. I speak now of etheric beings, spirit beings if you wish. They are not ordinarily visible to us. They belong, however, to the Earth Realm and they dwell in the atmospheric and etheric planes surrounding earth's surface. Now let us look "inside" our incredible planet.

- 6 -

"Incredible" is indeed the word for it. Incredible, mysterious, fascinating and awesome is the earth's interior. Jules Verne was fascinated enough by it to write a book titled: "Journey to The Center of the Earth". You can find a copy of the book in any library. Better yet, a movie film was made with that title, starring James Mason, Pat Boone and Arlene Dahl. If this picture comes your way again, by all means see it. It is wonderfully presented and faithful to the spirit in which the author wrote it. What is more, I am sure that Jules Verne wrote better than he knew.

In Verne's story, a scientist discovers a secret entrance leading down into the center of the earth. Through great labyrinthian caves in the mountains of Iceland, the courageous explorer leads his companions -- a young science student, a large Nordic farmer with his pet goose named "Gertrude", and a very lovely and dauntless woman whose scientist husband has recently died under mysterious circumstances. Down into the caves goes this group of three men and a woman--and a goose.

Exciting? You bet. And the excitement mounts with each passing second as the group continues to descend farther and farther into the interior of the earth. Great caves of beautiful crystals, all glowing with the radiance of various pastel colors are discovered by the bold explorer.

Deep pools of fluorescent water are found. Rocks dropped into the pools would cause the water to glow and sparkle with an eerie light. Much, much more is experienced by the adventurers in Jules Verne's story that makes it important reading for all New Age individuals. It is more than fiction.

Way back in 1895 another novel appeared that "rocked the foundations" of man's customary mode of thinking. The title of this book was "ETIDORPHA" (Aphrodite spelled backwards). It was written by John Uri Lloyd, who called his book "A Novel of Mystery". ETIDORPHA was issued privately in 1895. It was published by Dodd, Mead and Company of New York. Copies are scarce.

In his novel, John Uri Lloyd took the same point of view that Jules Verne did. Verne, for example, had one of his story characters say: "The inner earth is our next frontier. Man knows more about the workings of the stars than he knows about the very ground beneath his feet!"

"Man must yet search," said Lloyd in Etidorpha, "by the agency of senses and spirit, the UNFATHOMED MYSTERIES that lie beneath his feet and over his head, and he who refuses to bow to the Creator and honor His handiwork discredits himself.... When this work is accomplished, AS IT YET WILL BE, the future man, able then to comprehend the problem of life in its broader

- 7 -

significance -- drawing from all directions the facts necessary to his mental advancement -- will have reached a state in
which he can enjoy bodily comfort and supreme spiritual perfection, while yet a mortal.."

     Marshall B. Gardner wrote a book in 1913 in which he set
forth his theory of a hollow earth with "openings at the poles".
These polar orifices, he surmised, lead into the great unknown
(to us) country inside the earth. The book in which Gardner
presented his idea was titled: "A JOURNEY TO THE EARTH'S INTERIOR"
or "HAVE THE POLES REALLY BEEN DISCOVERED?". Luckily, I have a
copy of the book.

     His argument for a hollow earth is convincing:

     "Our theory may be untrue, but if it is, then the find-
ings of Nansen and every other Arctic explorer, of Sir Robert
Ball, Percival Lowell and every other astronomer, are wrong.
For upon the work done by these men and upon no other consider-
ations whatsoever than those of pure scientific knowledge are
the ideas in this book built.

     "Now as a matter of fact the scientists themselves no
longer hold the ideas about the constitution of the earth that
were taught in all text books only a few years ago. The notion
that the earth is a great ball of material which has hardened
into a shell or crust on the outside, but which is full of
molten material within, getting hotter and hotter as we reach
the center -- that notion IS NOW NO LONGER GENERALLY HELD. And
no other theory has quite taken its place.

     "Some think that while the earth may have a solid center
that it does have a liquid hot layer somewhere between its center and its surface. But NONE of the theories up to the present
have explained all the facts.

     "Of course it is very easy for anyone to deny all the
facts of science and get up some purely private explanation of
the formation of the earth. The man who does that is a crank..
..There is one man who has stated that the earth is an immense
hollow sphere and that mankind and the land and oceans and even
the stars ARE ALL ON THE INSIDE OF IT! But he is a crank for
he has simply taken his private notion, evolved within his own
brain and has made a religion of it. (NOTE: Dr. Cyrus R. Teed,
M.D. known as "Koresh", startled the world and his followers with
this strange theory in the early 1920's.--M.X.)

     "Nearly one hundred years ago in America a theory was put
forth that the earth consisted of a number of concentric spheres
one within the other. Now that could hardly be called a scientific theory. It was based on a supposition, and the author

- 8 -

argued from his supposition down to what the facts ought to be.
He said in effect, 'According to my principle there ought to
be within the earth a series of spheres each one inside the
other.' But he did not <u>know</u>, and he <u>never went down to see</u>.

"We take the opposite course. We begin with the facts.
We claim that the earth is A HOLLOW BODY with an immense opening at each polar axis -- an opening about 1400 miles in diameter -- and that there is in the interior of the earth a sun
which warms it and gives it light. We state that this formation
of a hollow shell around a central sun, with polar openings, is
not alone the formation of the earth but of every planetary body
throughout the stellar universe. Why do we say that? Because
we think it ought to be? Because we wish to impose our own idea
on to the facts? No, but because we can see these polar openings
and occasionally the gleam of the central sun as we look at Mars
or Venus through a telescope. And so it goes. The theory of
which we write is not so much a theory that we put forth as it is
a theory which the facts put forth to us when we examine them!"

COMMENT BY MICHAEL X: A hollow earth? Why not? The idea
isn't too surprising, and some of the evidence I shall include
in this Report is astonishing. The BIG THING, the really important thing is...IF the earth is hollow it may well be <u>inhabited</u>.
By whom? Living beings, human and otherwise! Frankly, from
what we've seen, heard and added-up in our own mind in recent
months, we believe the inner earth is not only inhabited by humans,
but by humans far more ADVANCED IN SCIENCE THAN WE ARE! And that
poses a very SERIOUS problem.

Follow me now in your imagination for a moment. Imagine a
race of fellow human beings dwelling far beneath the surface of
this earth, in a vast hollow interior region some 4,400 miles
in circumference. Figuring four directions, that is a lot of
land area. Population of the "Inner Earth" could be as large,
maybe larger than that of our outer earth.

Now suppose that race of people inside the earth are 500
to 1,000 years ahead of our nations in inventions. If that were
true, they'd have already perfected the kind of flying craft
that are most efficient...FLYING SAUCERS. And suppose they decided to "investigate" the outer earth where you and I are living. They'd come up through secret openings at the poles and
elsewhere, in their flying craft and we'd see in our skies FLYING
SAUCERS FROM INNER EARTH!

ooo0OO0ooo
- 9 -

Part 2

In the year 1947 Admiral Richard E. Byrd made a flight
into the South Polar region of the world. Before he started on
the venture, Byrd made a mysterious statement:

"I'd like to see that land BEYOND the Pole. That area
beyond the Pole is the center of the great unknown."

In the cockpit of his plane was a powerful, two-way radio.
When Byrd and his scientific companions took off from their
base at the South Pole, they managed to fly 1700 miles beyond
it. That's when the radio in Byrd's plane was put into use to
report something utterly incredible.

There was a strange great valley below them. For some
unknown reason, the valley Byrd saw was not ice-covered as it
should have been in the frigid Antarctic. It was green and
luxuriant. There were mountains with thick forests of trees
on them, there was lush grass and underbrush. Most amazing,
a huge animal was observed moving through the underbrush. In
a land of ice, snow and almost perpetual "deep-freeze"...here
was a stupendous MYSTERY.

Byrd had discovered a strange great valley just beyond
the South Pole, where the weather temperature, believe it or
not, was evidently something like 76 degrees!

Suddenly the press and radio were "hushed up". After
the first brief messages leaked through to newspapers, no further confirmation of the big discovery was given. Was it merely
a hoax? Some newsman's joke? I think not.

I believe that Byrd came upon the location of a great
doorway or entrance leading deep into the unknown interior of
this earth! The "Great Door" at the South Pole region. Having
found that, I believe he guessed no longer. He then KNEW beyond the shadow of a doubt that this secret "Door" must open
into the Cavern World.

He would go there and find out...see for himself the wonder and everlasting mystery of the unknown INNER earth.

On April 5, 1955, Admiral Richard E. Byrd was commissioned
by the U. S. Navy to explore the South Pole. One year later, from
the South Pole base, the U.S. Navy flew BEYOND the Pole to a
distance of 2300 miles. In this dramatic exploratory flight I
believe the Secret Great Door was seen.

Why believe that? Because Byrd's report on March 13, when
he returned from the South Pole was,"The present expedition has

- 10 -

opened up a vast NEW LAND." But you and I were never told exactly what Byrd and his men discovered. Why not? Was there a very good reason NOT to talk about it?

Frank Edwards, a serious UFO researcher, author and deep student of the Spacecraft phenomenon, wrote an article in the July, 1958 issue of Fate Magazine. Quote:

"In Admiral Richard Byrd's report of his first trip to the Antarctic his group discovered two large, blue-green lakes of warm water in the very midst of that desolate expanse of eternal ice. There was no trace of any volcanic heat supply, in fact, there was no visible means which could explain the incongruous co-existence of warm water lakes in the ice cap of the Antarctic. Admiral Byrd made note of still another strange aspect of the lakes. Alongside one of them, he wrote, were long, straight, black lines 'which resembled blast marks'."

Blast marks? Could some nation on earth be using the South Pole as a launching place for satellites or missiles? Doubtful. More likely the Inner Earth people are involved.

Richard Byrd reported the discovery of a large, warm water sea near the South Pole and stretching beyond it. The year was 1955. I think he also found something else. Something he could not speak about for special reasons. I think he found a mighty canyon bordering that warm sea...a canyon sloping gradually into the interior of the earth. Into the "Great Unknown Country" of the Inner Earth!

The Antarctic continent is big, terribly big. It is probably considerably larger than the former estimate of some 6,000,000 square miles of ice and snow. Results of the 1958 International Geophysical Year (IGY) of exploration indicate that the earth is covered with 40 per cent more ice than we'd previously estimated. Also, that Antarctica may be DIVIDED.

Now we have something! Science News Letter for January 17, 1959 carried this startling piece of information:

"Several discoveries increase the possibility that Antarctica may be divided in TWO. These include discovery of a sub-sea-level trough trending inland from Ellsworth Station, another trough on the opposite side of the continent trending inland from the Ross Sea and a deep basin in Marie Byrd Land."

If Antarctica IS divided, what does that mean? That there is another portion of that continent that nobody is telling us about? Does it mean there is another continent entirely -- a new land area -- in some unexplored sea? Possibly. If so, important information obviously has been withheld from the public.

- 11 -

How curiously strange that only recently, February 16th, 1960, four long years after Byrd's trip to the South Pole, this article was released to the newspapers:

"UNEXPLORED SEA ENTERED BY U.S. NAVY. Aboard the USS Glacier off Antarctica, Feb. 16, (UPI) - Two U.S. Navy ice-breakers today penetrated the Bellinghausen Sea for the first time in History and moved toward a stretch of Eastern Antarctica never before seen by man." (Emphasis is mine. MX)

Never before seen by man? I w-o-n-d-e-r! To stir up matters a little more, and "educate" us (the general public) gradually to the whole fantastic idea of an INNER EARTH and SAUCERS that come from there, here is another clipping that is loaded with dynamite. It appeared on the very same day that the "Unexplored Sea" bit was released:

SKY MYSTERY OVER ALASKA CONFIRMED. Colorado Springs, Feb. 16, (AP) - A spokesman for the North American Air Defense Command here confirmed today that unidentified flying objects were observed in the skies over Alaska early yesterday (2/16/60)

"The spokesman said at 3 a.m. yesterday the combat operations center of Norad at Ent Air Force Bast here received a report from northerly observation posts that two objects were moving in opposite directions across Alaska.

"One of the objects was reported in the vicinity of Nome. It appeared to be moving slowly in a northeasterly direction. The object disappeared without a trace and without giving any indication of its size."

Saucers over Alaska. Significant? Very. Both Alaska and Canada have had much more than their share of sightings in recent months. Why? Is there some connection with the "land beyond the Pole" -- that Unknown Country which we suspect is nothing less than THE INNER EARTH itself?

Indeed there is a connection. If the Saucers enter and leave the Inner Earth by way of the polar entrances, quite naturally they'd be seen by Alaskans and Canadians much more frequently than they would by people in other parts of the world. Alaska is close to the North Pole. So is Canada.

Every riddle has its answer. When Admiral Byrd went into the Unknown Country, into the center of the great unknown, where was he? If Marshall Gardner were here now I'm sure he'd agree with us when we gently suggest that Byrd was at the very doorway of the inner earth. In the South Pole area it lies beyond the Pole. But where?   In the South Pole area it may be found I feel reasonably certain, in Eastern Antarctica, that fabulous region "never before seen by man!"

- 12 -

I used to scoff at legends. I don't any more. Behind
every legend, strange to say, can be found a kernel of truth, a
group of facts around which the legend was built. That's why I
took the seeming legend of Rainbow City with a straight face,
and without a single grain of salt. Such a City is said to
exist. It's location? On the Eastern coast of the strange
Antarctic continent. I've included a map here on this page for
your study. It shows the approximate location of Rainbow City
...in Antarctica.

Antarctic Circle

So. Magnetic
Pole

O South
Pole

Atlantic
Ocean

ANTARCTICA

△ Rainbow City

The first CREDIBLE UFO (Unidentified Flying Object) sighting ever made in twentieth-century Antarctica is credited to
Chile's naval officer, Commander Augusto Orrego.

On March 12, 1950, confirmatory word of this sighting
reached saucercraft enthusiasts in Buffalo, New York. The exciting news was released on that day that Commander Orrego and
his men had spotted a fleet of rotund aerial machines circling
their Antarctic base. (Rainbow City. MX) A portion of the
Chilean officer's report told this amazing story:

"During the bright Antarctic night, we saw FLYING SAUCERS,
one above the other, turning at tremendous speeds. We have photographs to prove what we saw."

It seems that Rainbow City is more than a legend. It is
evidently entirely real...the secret base in mysterious Antarctica, for a fleet of SAUCERS coming from the center (we suspect)
of our own fantastic earth. Now let us go deeper, dear friend,
into the unexplored -- until we, like Admiral Byrd, will have
stepped into the CENTER of the Great Unknown,"beyond the Beyond".

oooOOOooo
- 13 -

THE REMARKABLE FINDING OF "BUNGER'S OASIS" IN ANTARCTICA!*

IS THE FABULOUS "RAINBOW CITY" LOCATED HERE?

In February of 1947, a most remarkable discovery was made in the continent of Antarctica. This discovery is known now as "Bunger's Oasis". Lt. Commander David Bunger was at the controls of one of the six large transport planes used by Admiral Byrd for the U. S. Navy's "Operation Highjump". (1946-47)

Bunger was flying inland from the Shackleton Ice Shelf, near the Queen Mary Coast of Wilkes Land. He and his crew were about four miles from the coastline where open water lies.

For two months previous to this moment, all that Bunger and his flight crew had seen below was white polar wasteland. In one dramatic second all that monotony vanished. Suddenly they could see a large dark spot of land up ahead of them...an area some three hundred square miles in size. It seemed to be completely free of snow or ice. And it had many lakes.

The land itself was ice-free. The lakes were of many different colors, ranging from rusty red, green, to deep blues. The strange thing about the colors is that they were bright as though something in the water caused them to attract more light. Each of the lakes was more than three miles long. The water was warmer than the ocean, as Bunger soon found by landing his seaplane on one of the lakes. Each lake had a gently sloping beach.

Around the four edges of the Oasis, which was roughly square in shape, Bunger saw endless and eternal white snow and ice. Two sides of the Oasis rose nearly one hundred feet high, and consisted of great ice walls. The other two sides had a more gradual and gentle slope.

I believe that this "Oasis" of unfrozen territory is not the result of hot volcanic activity beneath the surface of the land. Three hundred square miles is simply too big an area to be affected by volcanic heat supply, although that could account for some of the ice-free land. A Secret Door, not as large as some theorists(such as Marshall Gardner) thought, could well be located somewhere in that vast territory. Warm currents from the Cavern World could be circulating from that opening.

Rainbow City could be located at Bunger's Oasis. Multicolored lakes certainly remind one of the rainbow, and could be the real explanation back of the city's name. The City itself is most likely near the opening that leads into the underground cities. By now, the major portion of the city's structures may have been removed from the surface and taken inside for greater security. This is entirely possible. The outer surface of the great valley would still serve as a perfect spacecraft base.

*Note: Ref.   - 13-a -
The Silent Continent - Kearns
(Harper & Bros. 1955)

Chapter 3

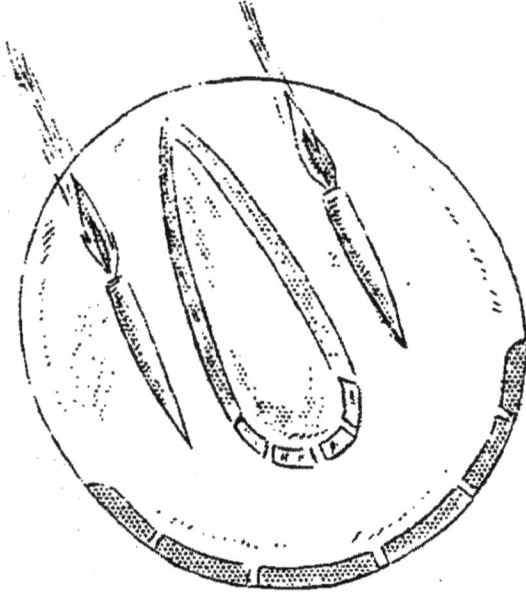

A Rainbow City Saucer

The idea of people living in the interior of the earth is not new. Belief in the existence of an advanced race of people dwelling inside our earth is, in fact, quite ancient. In all the ancient teachings of various races--the Greeks, Norwegians, Aztecs, Mayans, Hindus, Egyptians etc., etc.--we find stories about "Inner Earth" people.

You may recall the theme of the Egyptian Book of The Dead. A strange and mysterious boatman had charge of the souls of the newly departed. The boat would either transport the human soul up into the region of the stars, or...if the soul needed more basic training or possibly stern discipline, the boatman would pilot the souls silently along the River Styx. The River of course, led deep down into the interior of the earth.

All the churches I know about have a concept of some place or region called "Hell".* Catholics refer to a sort of "in-between" place known as "purgatory" or "limbo" for souls. The Bible mentions "Hades", "Gehenna", "Tartaros" and "Sheol". All four terms apparently mean the same thing...a region within the earth where human beings go if they should be so unlucky as not to make the grade on the outside of the earth. The idea of Inner Earth dwellers is by no means new.

What is new is this: Some of those inner earth people are evidently far ahead of outer earth people in their inventions and scientific technology. After more than twelve years of UFO investigation I have concluded this is so. If you consider the extremely ancient lineage of the inner earth dwellers, it's easy to admit this. These beings were on earth before the great flood!

Who then, are the inner earth people? Just as on the surface of the earth, you'll doubtless find that in the earth's interior are not one, but SEVERAL different races and types of people. There may be found pygmies, midgets, and dwarfs. Also there may be found average sized human beings like you and me. But most important...and the significance of this is absolutely worldshaking...there may be found GIANTS living inside the earth!

*Note: "Hell" can, of course, be defined metaphysically as merely the negative experience on the road to truth, but we exclude this.

- 14 -

GIANTS? Yes, giants. I'll admit it sounds like something out of Hans Christian Andersen's story book, but what are
the facts? Upon what do we base our statement regarding giants?

It happened a long time ago, the strangest story of them
all..the coming of the giants. They are directly related to a
wise and powerful race of outer space people which the Bible
calls the "Sons of God". They did not make their home on the
earth originally, instead they invaded this planet from outer
space and took it over as their own.

"And it came to pass, when men began to multiply on the
face of the earth, and daughters were born unto them, that the
Sons of God saw the daughters of men that they were fair; and
they took them wives of all which they chose.

"There were giants in the earth in those days; and also
after that, when the sons of God came in unto the daughters of
men, the same became mighty men which were of old, men of re-
nown...The earth also was corrupt before God; and the earth was
filled with violence. And God looked upon the earth, and behold
it was corrupt; for all flesh had corrupted his way upon the
earth." (Gen. 6:1-4, 11-12)

Then came the sudden "balancing of the cosmic books".
A flood, a mighty Deluge was unloosed upon the earth and we are
told it rained for forty long days and forty long nights.

What happened to the giants? Did they all perish in the
great flood? I do not think so. Those giants were the offspring
of outer-space men and outer-earth women. They were "hybrids",
just as the little pygmies were also "hybrids". But those outer
space people and their children were not as dull-witted as to
take no action for their own survival.

Sensing in advance, as they must have, what was coming,
the intelligent race of outer-space people took their hybrid
offspring (giants and pygmies) OFF the surface of the earth!

A mighty Exodus! To where? Into the center of the earth,
where they could find protection from the big Deluge. Just before the Flood then, in the days of Noah, those amazing human
beings who had invaded this earth from outer space..went into
the Inner Earth in a mass migration, and are still there. That
is, their offspring are most likely there now, and with their
inheritance of space flight "know-how", they are--and have been
since 1947--coming out in spacecraft. They have "Saucers"!

The Bible clearly states that there are people above the
earth, on the earth, and in the earth. (Rev. 5:3 & 13) If
people live inside the hollow earth, it is only logical to sup-

- 15 -

pose that in due time--as they progress in science and invention
--they will get around to visiting us. After all, we outer-
earth dwellers are looking forward to visiting our neighboring
planets, Mars, Venus, etc. Only thing that's holding us back is
that we don't have spaceships perfected enough to get us to those
other planets safely. That, plus our immature attitude of conquest.

In other words, we haven't progressed scientifically e-
nough at this present time. We need more time. Whereas, on the
other hand, the inner earth people have been carrying on from
the point where their outer-space ancestors left off. That, at
least, is our working theory.

They could be 1,000 or more years in advance of our own
technology, and from the looks of things, they are now and have
been for some time...looking us over carefully.

In antediluvian times -- that is, before the Flood -- our
planet probably had more land surface than it has today. In
those days, our earth's surface probably had EQUAL PARTS land
and water. A huge watery Canopy or "envelope" hung suspended
above the earth, very much like the strange thick cloud formation that is seen today around the planet Venus.

With less water on the earth, with less oceans and with a
much more Edenic temperature at the North and South Poles than
we have now, the "Great Doors" or openings leading into the interior of the earth were relatively EASY to locate.

But times have changed...drastically. So have climatic
conditions everywhere on this troubled planet of ours. When the
earth tilted on its axis thousands of years ago, the Watery Canopy above the earth broke, causing the great Deluge or Flood.
It also virtually CONCEALED the OPENINGS at the poles. Not only
were both poles surrounded by thousands of square miles of frigid ice, snow and stormy weather, which made the Great Doors terribly difficult to get to...but there was still another difficulty.
DIRECTIONAL DIFFICULTY...!

Near either of the poles any explorer is apt to lose his
bearings quite easily, as the magnetic compass becomes completely
erratic. Today, the invention of the "Gyro-compass" enables a
ship to keep its location calculated in the Arctic and Antarctic.
In early days, however, say back as far as 1894 when Fridtjof
Nansen went looking for the North Pole, he not only failed to
find it...He got so lost that he wrote in his diary: "We do not
know where we are, and we do not know when this will end." Where
was he? Nansen hadn't the slightest idea. He wandered with his
crew for an entire summer and winter in the Arctic, completely
LOST. His compass? It pointed restlessly in most any direction!
It spun round and round at times, but it was no help at all.

- 16 -

Finally, Nansen and his men made the right turn somehow, and got out of the "strange land" that he had gotten so lost in. I strongly suspect that he was lost on the outer lip or edge of the Great Door leading into the "Unknown Country". Had he not been successful in backtracking, he might have gone into the inner regions of this earth..and be there yet!

Where is Rainbow City? In the vastness of Antarctica, near its eastern coast...some 2300 miles from the South Pole. What is it? A secret city owned by the Inner Earth people, and used as a base for their Flying Saucers. Incredible! It is located, we believe, not inside the Great Door, but fairly close to that "Door" yet outside of it.

In spite of what we have always imagined about the inner earth being the abode of bad and wicked people, those assumptions might not be entirely true. There are good and bad people IN the inner earth, and the same thing is true on the surface of the earth. Quite true, many of the Rainbow People may be giants. Ten, twelve, eighteen feet tall, some of them. But there are "friendly giants" among them. In fact, they may all be more friendly and advanced in spiritual matters than we know.

Now hold onto that chair you are sitting in, and I will tell you a real "giant" story! I got the story from my close friend, Dr. "C" whom I introduced to you in a previous book I wrote called "Venusian Health Magic".

Dr. "C" in real life is known as Dr. Nephi Cottam, D.C. of Los Angeles. Recently he had as one of his patients, a man of Nordic descent who I shall not mention by name at this time. This Nordic individual is, however, entirely real. He told the following story to Nephi. Here it is just as he told it:

"I live near the Arctic circle, in Norway. One summer my friend and I made up our minds to take a boat trip together, and go as far as we could into the North country. So we put one month's food provisions into a small fishing boat and with sail and also a good engine in our boat, set out to sea.

"At the end of one month we had traveled far into the north, beyond the pole and into a strange new country. We were much astonished at the weather there. Warm, and at times at night it was almost too warm to sleep. Then we saw something so strange we both were astounded. Ahead of the warm, open sea we were on, was what looked like a great mountain. Into that mountain at a certain point, the ocean seemed to be emptying. Mystified, we continued in that direction and found ourselves sailing into a vast canyon leading into the interior of the earth. We kept sailing and then saw what surprised us--a sun shining inside the earth!

- 17 -

"The ocean that had carried us into the hollow interior of the earth, gradually became a river. This river leads, as we came to realize later...all through the inner surface of the world from one end to the other. It can take you, if you follow it long enough, from the North Pole clear through to the South Pole.

"We saw that the inner earth's surface was divided, even as the outer one is, into both land and water. There is plenty of sunshine, and both animal and vegetable life abound there. We sailed further and further into this fantastic country... fantastic because everything was huge in size as compared to things on the outside. Plants were big, trees gigantic, and then we came upon the GIANTS.

"They were dwelling in homes and towns just as we do on the earth's surface. And they used a type of electrical conveyance like a mono-rail car, to transport people. It ran along the river's edge from town to town.

"Several of the inner earth inhabitants--huge giants-- detected our boat on the river, and were quite amazed. They seemed just as astonished to see us as we were to see them! They were, however, quite friendly. We were invited to dine with them in their homes, and so my companion and I separated --he going with one giant to that giant's home, and I going with another giant to his home.

"My gigantic friend brought me home to his family, and I was completely dismayed to see the huge size of all of the objects in his home. The dinner table was colossal. A plate was put before me and filled with a portion of food so big it would have fed me abundantly for an entire week! The giant offered me a cluster of grapes and each grape was as big as one of our outer-earth peaches. I tasted one and found it far sweeter than any I had ever tasted "outside". In the inner earth all the fruits and vegetables taste far better and more flavorsome than those we have on the outer earth.

"We stayed with the giants for one year, enjoying their companionship as much as they enjoyed knowing us. We observed many strange and unusual things during our visit with these remarkable people, and were continuelly amazed at their scientific progress and inventions. All of this time they were never unfriendly to us, and we were allowed to return to our own home in the same manner in which we had come--in fact, they courteously offered their protection if we should need it for the return voyage."

oooOOOooo

- 18 -

Chapter 4

Atlantis

For a moment, let us reserve our judgment as to whether or not we believe in the existence of a race of giants dwelling inside the hollow of the earth. Another very interesting problem is now facing us. It is highly important because it "ties-in" strangely with the existence of Inner Earth people.

The problem is, what really happened to Colonel Percy Harrison Fawcett, who disappeared into the Brazilian Jungle over thirty years ago? He was searching, you may recall, for traces of a long-lost Atlantean Civilization.

Stories and rumors innumerable have arisen through the years seeking to explain his disappearance, but none have proven conclusive and the "mystery" remains unsolved.

In the Spring of 1925 Col. Fawcett set out upon his last Brazilian expedition. With him were his son Jack and a young friend named Raleigh Rimell. Into the dread Matto Grosso area of Brazil went the brave expedition. They were looking for a "secret city" built by the people of Atlantis when Atlantis was in its "heyday". Col. Fawcett was no stranger to the "green hell of the great Brazilian jungles. Between 1906 and 1921 he had led four expeditions into the Matto Grosso.

But on his fifth expedition he vanished completely. The last historical fact known about him and his companions is that received by his wife in a letter from Fawcett, on May 29th, 1925. He'd reached Dead Horse Camp, he wrote. His next objective was a waterfall which he hoped to reach in a week or ten days. No further letters were ever written by Fawcett to his wife, nor were the explorers ever seen on the "outer earth" again.

Was Col. Fawcett aware of the existence of an advanced race of people who lived in the hollow center of the earth? Is it possible that Brazilian Navy Commander Justino Strauss may be right in his strong suspicion that, "...these mysterious engines (flying saucers) come from the center of the earth, where it has long been believed that life exists to a degree far advanced over our own civilization." Commander Strauss felt that in some way Colonel Fawcett's disappearance was connected with the mysterious operations of the Inner Earth people.

- 19 -

The riddle of Atlantis is also involved here. To this
day, nobody -- with the possible exception of a rare few individuals who can read the "Memory of Nature" -- knows for sure
whether or not there ever was a real Atlantis. Plato, the
famous Greek philosopher gave us this amazing account:

"....Our (Egyption) histories tell of a mighty power
(Atlantis) which was aggressing wantonly against the whole of
Europe and Asia, and to which your city (Athens) put an end.
This power came forth out of the Atlantic Ocean for in those
days the Atlantic was navigable; and there was an island situ-
ated in front of the straits which you call the Pillars of
Hercules (the Straits of Gibraltar).

"The island was larger than Libya and Asia put together.
...now in this island there was a great and wonderful empire
which had the rule over the whole island and several others as
well as over parts of the continent. And besides these, they
subjected the parts of Libya within the Pillars of Hercules
as far as Egypt, and of Europe as far as Tyrrhenia (Italy).

"...In later times there occurred violent EARTHQUAKES and
FLOODS, and in a single day and night of rain all the war-like
men in a body sank into the earth, and the island of Atlantis
in a like manner disappeared and was sunk beneath the sea."

Now here it comes...the shocker. I believe that Atlantis
was every bit real, and that the Atlanteans' ancestors are living today, now, in the interior of the earth. They are in all
probability very large people, physically. Perhaps blonde*
giants. But why believe they are still in existence?

Because persistent rumors have it that a vast system of
subterranean TUNNELS exist beneath the land of South America.
Secret openings are said to exist, leading from the surface of
the earth into the tunnels. In his book "Agharta", Robert E.
Dickhoff claims that a fantastic network of tunnels exists
underground. These tunnels radiate outward from the Antarctic
area (from Rainbow City we suspect) to every other continent
on earth! This would, naturally, include Atlantis which had
not been submerged at the time those tunnels were built.

According to Dickhoff, one tunnel surfaces in the Matto
Grosso region of Brazil...precisely where Col. Fawcett vanished
in 1925! Another tunnel has its opening in Kentucky, (the great
Mammoth Cave perhaps) another in a southwestern state.(FLASH:
A new cave said to be one thousand times larger than Carlsbad
Caverns has been reported discovered in Arizona!) And other
tunnels are said to surface in Tibet and in the Pacific Ocean.

*(We know of persons who have had vivid "Inner Earth" dreams in
which they saw blonde giants.)

- 20 -

Now if you were "hot on the trail" of Col. Percy Fawcett
and his men and all those explorers who set out to search for
him later and who also disappeared...you'd wonder about those
tunnels wouldn't you? Who originally built them and why.

Robert Dickhoff surmises that a race of outer-space invaders built the tunnels, long before the great Noaic Deluge.
They were Martians, he suspects. Martians who came to earth
and colonized it many thousands of years ago; but they were war-
like and built the tunnels as a great defensive system in case
of atomic or interplanetary war.

Rainbow City, says Dickhoff, was one of seven magnificent
cities built by the outer-space invaders. All the cities were
encased in ice...miles of ice...when the earth tilted and the
Flood came. All the cities, that is, except one. Rainbow City
was near the opening, the Great Door leading into the interior
of the earth. Warmth from the interior world kept Rainbow City
from freezing over. The Rainbow City people most likely still
use that City as a spaceship base.

Two contemporary scientists have declared that the ruins
of Atlantis are not on the ocean floor, but at the city of
Tiahuanaco in the Andes Mountains of South America. I think
what they are really trying to say is that the Atlanteans moved
at least a small remnant of their civilization to South America
before the vast cataclysm engulfed their Island empire.

In 1935 a well-known medium in London by the name of
Geraldine Cummins began communication with Col. Percy Fawcett
by means of extrasensory perception. A steady flow of messages,
all assertedly from Fawcett, were written down by Geraldine
automatically--with almost super-speed. She recorded these
communications faithfully, and published them in 1955 in a book
entitled, "The Fate of Colonel Fawcett". (The Aquarian Press,
London.) The messages brought out the idea that the explorer
had passed on into another realm, that he was no more in our
"earthly world".

It is certainly possible that Col. Fawcett died in the
wilds of Brazil. In fact, all of the explorers who plunged so
recklessly into the green jungles of the Matto Grosso, could
very easily have been killed by Indians there. Or the swampy
jungle itself could have beaten them. I've been in jungles
myself. Most of them are bad...unhealthy, fever-ridden.

But Col. Fawcett knew those conditions well. He'd led
FOUR previous expeditions, remember, into the Matto Grosso. On
his fifth trip, it is possible that he did meet with success.
Perhaps he found the "secret city"..and MORE. A tunnel nearby
leading down into the earth's fantastic cavern kingdoms, and may
be the people there never permitted him to leave.

oooOOOooo
- 21 -

Chapter 5

Why was Col. Fawcett so anxious to discover the "lost cities" of the Atlanteans in Brazil? Because of its TREASURE. The Treasure of the Sun God was hidden in those ancient ruins and that treasure was not simply GOLD, but something else of much greater importance. Some power called "Blast-electricity".

The Sun God's real secret, then, according to the psychic communications which Geraldine Cummins received, was not gold, but a power. A power men would give kingdoms to gain. It was derived from the sun, and Fawcett termed it "Blast Electricity".

On December 7th, 1935, Geraldine received this message:

"When I set out on that expedition to find the pyramids, (Atlantean) a number of people said, and many thought, that I was crazy. But I am nothing of the sort. If we are to continue, you must believe in my sanity. You must accept my assurance that the last relics of an ancient civilization, Egyptian in character, are to be found in central South America. (Egypt was really a colony of lesser Atlanteans who started colonies in other parts of the earth). With my living eyes I have seen these ruins...I believe that, if the climate were not so oppressive and we could bring gangs of men here, excavating under skilled direction, a whole ancient civilization would be revealed--the SECRET of the Lost Continent would be divulged, a flood of light thrown on a period that is pre-historic, and our origins more clearly realized. What is more, these races were as civilized as are the Europeans of today. Only they travelled on a different orientation.

"Sun worship was the basic principle on which the whole of this central American Civilization was founded. Now this is important. (Attention, dear readers, this is IT! M.X)

"I want to get at the secret of the sun-power," said the indomitable explorer, "for to me it is the finest adventure upon which I have entered so far!

"Listen! You don't know, no living man knows, what electricity is. These Atlanteans knew more or less the nature of electricity, which is dependent on the SUN, yet is also allied to other air forces. Of course, there is more than one kind of electricity. The kind that is known to men was discovered by the Atlanteans, but they used their kind of electricity in a DIFFERENT way from us.

"They realized that it might be used, not merely to give light--queer globular lights--but that it might also be employed

- 22 -

in connection with the SHIFTING OF WEIGHTS. The building of
the Pyramids is solved when you know that huge blocks of stone
can be manipulated through what I call blast-electricity.

"You will think me mad when I talk of electrified winds,
for you know nothing about the CONNECTION between air and electricity, the alliance between it and LIGHT. Terms like the
compression of air and the accumulation of electricity for the
purpose of COMBINING THE TWO--so that what is solid may be removed, have not yet entered into the imagination of man. But
I, who have seen this ancient world, walked its streets, halted
before the porticoes of its temples (HERE IT COMES!)(M.X.)...
DESCENDED INTO THE GREAT SUBTERRANEAN WORLD wherein electricity
and air are combined and fused, can assure you that the men who
came before modern history was recorded..knew more about matter
and light, about the ether and its properties, than the scientists of the twentieth century can ever know or imagine!

          (COMMENT BY MICHAEL X: Go over that sentence once more,
"I, who have....descended into the GREAT SUBTERRANEAN WORLD..".
Into the Inner Earth? What a bombshell!)

          "Picture to yourself wide reservoirs of compressed elec-
trified air reclaimed and stored in HUGE POCKETS under the surface of the earth. Coal mines! Oh, yes, I know all about the
miles of burrows.. under Welsh soil. But these are nothing when
compared with the STORAGE BATTERIES (tunnels and caverns) that
were like some vast design existing under the solid crust of
soil, and were guarded and maintained by an army of Atlanteans.

          "But this is what I am getting at. It was man, and not
the forces of nature, that destroyed Atlantis. Or rather, men
developed to such a degree these subterranean storehouses of
electrified air, that at last it revolted and pitched man and
the solid earth heavenward. Then GREAT WAS THE FALL. Seas
flowed in over the disintegrated, sunken land. Thousands of
miles of country were submerged--('in a single day and night'
says Plato in his written account titled TIMAEUS)--and earth
thrown up in other places formed new countries.

          "I don't think your scientists have the imagination to
conceive the principles of electrified air--and I hope they
never will. For you must understand that it can be used as a
destructive weapon--extremely dangerous because it is invisible.
Blast-electricity was an undoubted fact. It is a fact too dangerous to disclose to your generation--I mean the secret of the
process employed to produce and maintain this tremendous force.
(NOTE BY MICHAEL X: This was NOT atomic power, though possibly
a few Atlanteans knew how to split the atom. Blast-electricity
was no doubt more easily obtained from sun and air.)

          "We on earth know how to generate electricity from coal

- 23 -

and from water power. These ancients went much further. They
had devised an instrument that could extract from the all-per-
vading atmosphere the electricity necessary to all the concerns
of their life. (Known as FREE-ENERGY to the space people. M.X.)
They used these massed electrons for a thousand different purposes. These not only heated and lighted their dwellings --
they moved great weights. Instruments were devised which automatically performed functions such as cooking, serving and
cleaning in households. Furthermore, they were used for..defense.

"Eventually they were able to conserve this massed sun-
power to such an extent that, when WAR broke out, they fired
too violently and suddenly what I might call their 'electrified
projectiles'. The chambers of compressed electricity were suddenly rent asunder, a vast cataclysm followed, and -- as I have
previously described to you -- the face of the world was changed
by these convulsions."

The Sun-power had many other functions in Atlantis besides
that of destruction, as Col. Fawcett noted previously. He felt
that in time he would discover the Sun-God's secret, and make
use of it not to dominate and enslave man, but to benefit him.
"I explained to Raleigh," said the Colonel, "that if we could
discover the formula for this force, and then convey it by Indian
messages to my wife, who was in Peru, she would return with it
to London. There she would give the paper on which was written the secret method of production of the power,to the right
people and we would indeed bestow IMMENSE BENEFIT ON MANKIND. I
was thinking then solely of its possibilities for fertilization,
for obtaining QUADRUPLE YIELDS from the land. Above all, I was
confident that soil, worn out and used up by wheat crops, could
be turned into virgin soil by this means.

"For it has seemed to me that in our own day the primary
cause of WAR is the menace of hunger to over-numerous virile
races. This rouses an instinctive, primitive desire to acquire
the wheat lands of their neighbors. I said to Raleigh: "There
must not be another 1914-1918 war. We may possibly be able to
prevent such a calamity if we find one of the uses of the Sun-
force--that of immensely increasing the supply of food from a
given area of land."

Astounding! Perfectly astounding! So that's why our
friend Col. Percy Fawcett FIVE TIMES searched the dangerous jungles of Brazil. FREE-ENERGY! That's what he really wanted to
find there in those pre-historic ruins of the LostCity. A discovery SO BIG it could, rightly used, END WAR FOREVER. It could
make our present money system obsolete almost overnight! Destiny
however, decreed otherwise, Mankind was not quite ready for the
super-potent force known as the Secret of the Sun God, and if
Fawcett did learn the formula, he was never permitted to reveal
it.

oooOOOooo
- 24 -

Chapter 6

Now dear friend, let's continue this tremendous "New Age Adventure" together. Who knows but that you and I might uncover startling new truths bigger than "both of us" and I think we may start by asking, "Why the hush-hush about the flying saucers?" "Why the policy of governmental SECRECY?"

Not too long ago I received a letter from a sincere spacecraft investigator, a lady I know and enjoy talking with. Her letter hit the nail exactly on the head. I quote:

"Just why the Government won't tell the people the truth is beyond me. Do they actually know? They claim that the people would panic...WHY? Is there any reason to panic, and what do they base the word 'panic' upon? Are the Space Beings like us, that is in shape and form? Michael, any additional advice will be greatly appreciated..and thank you so much..."

For years I did not know the answers to these questions, because my experience had to do with "Outer-Space beings" only. Venusians. I'd learned that the people of Venus are in no sense warlike, that they consider us their younger brothers and sisters and wish to help us step into a higher vibration.

What then, is the secret reason for hush-hush? I believe the reason for secrecy regarding the saucer people is due to our Government's knowledge of "Inner Earth" people! I have a strong hunch that our military got a good look at Rainbow City during Admiral Byrd's expedition to the "land beyond the pole" in Antarctica back in 1956! Rainbow City, we've reasoned, is a space base for Inner Earth dwellers. Speaking plainly, I am talking about "Giants" who have flying saucers!

Now a "Giant" is nothing more than a human being who has grown large, perhaps two or three times our size. A well-proportioned giant is usually physically strong, but that doesn't necessarily make him an "ogre"...something to be feared, dreaded or destroyed.

In the Southern California desert area, reports of "Giants" have been springing up over a period of many months. Dr. W. C. Halsey who lives not too far from my home in Los Angeles, has had more than 60 reports of sightings of Giants brought to his attention. In his "COLLEGE OF KNOWLEDGE NEWS LETTER", Feb. 1960, Vol. 1, No. 6, Dr. Halsey writes, "Most of these reports were from a semi-official source, or I should say the official source was speaking off the cuff. One instance was that of a personal acquaintance. At no time were these Giants posing a real threat. Although our military was scared beyond words at their sight,

not because of reason really, but because they were GIANTS.
Many people take a dim view of these reports. However, there are
too many reports from too many parts of the world to call it
nonsense."

From a South American source, Dr. Halsey recently received
the following two reports of Giant Saucer People:

1. Three witnesses looking across a valley (due to this
reason they could not approach), saw two men of great height
climbing a slope with their backs to the observers. This was
at 9:00 A.M. The two strange beings wore brilliant red clothing
from head to foot; they were well proportioned and walked with
a normal pace seeming to ignore the presence of the witnesses.
When they walked near some trees it was then possible to calcu-
late their height: one of them measured 5 or 6 meters, and the
other about 3 meters.

(A meter is 39.37 U.S. inches, making the taller man
around 19 feet 6 inches, and "shorty" was only about 9 feet, 8
inches.) A member of our society (W.B.) investigated this case
and it was reported to him that: two hours earlier, before the
"Giants" appeared, a merchant and his family, initials C.M., saw
a luminous, polished round object moving in the skies toward the
place where the "Giants" were seen two hours later. The merchant's sighting was at a neighboring town.

2. Some time prior to this period, 7 men of small height
"looking like children", were seen in Quebra Coco near Ceres by
two witnesses. These men emerged from the entrance door of a
HUGE SAUCER "200 meters in diameter by 15 meters high, with an
antenna measuring 30 meters long." For three minutes they observed the witnesses in silence. End quote.

In report (2) the 7 men of small height who resembled
children, might very well BE children. The natural offspring
of giant adults, getting a good look at "outer earth" people!

By the way, you'd enjoy reading Dr. Halsey's "NEWSLETTER"
regularly. It will certainly keep you "right up to the minute"
on Spacecraft news, latest info on the "Giants" and other very
important things you should know about. I highly recommend it.
Write direct to Dr. and Mrs. W. C. Halsey, 731 So. Serrano Ave.,
Los Angeles 5, Calif. Request "NEWSLETTER" and enclose $1.00.

Getting back to the questions asked me in that letter from
the lady correspondent, we may now answer them one by one. (1)
Does the Government actually know the truth? Ans: If you mean
the truth that some of the flying saucers may be coming from
inside this earth, and that their pilots may be Giants, YES...I
think the Government (s) are fully aware of this. As you and I

- 25 -

know, President Eisenhower quite recently (February) visited
Sao Paulo, Brazil to see our South American friends. We know
that a secret entrance, an opening into a tunnel that leads
down into the Inner Earth kingdom, is purported to exist some
where in the Matto Grosso region of Brazil.

And we also know Brazil is worried...about SAUCERS! So
many flying saucers are coming out of Brazil--flying around the
cities there--that the Brazilian government in the state of
Sao Paulo recently formed a special committee. Purpose? To
study the PROBLEM of flying saucers!

"During a 14 month period, no less than 149 sightings
were officially reported in Brazil," reports Dr. Halsey in his
Newsletter. "In 44 of these cases they were seen by local authorities. In 27 cases whole communities of hundreds of people
sighted the objects at the same time. In 7 cases it was possible
to take photographs. In all instances there was excitement to
say the least."

I am only "thinking out loud", but I'd say there is a
definite "tie-in" between the increase of saucer sightings in
Brazil, the secret tunnels in South America, the reports of
"Giants" seen with flying saucers, and Ike's visit to Brazil.

(2) "They claim the public would panic." Ans. I have no
doubt that they would. Giants are somewhat sensational.

(3) "Are the Space beings like us, in shape and form?"
Ans: Yes. They look like us. Venusians are about 6 feet in
height on the average. Size varies. That's the trouble in the
case of Inner Earth people. They're so gigantic we are liable
to assume at once that they're unfriendly or dangerous. And
yet the fact is, they haven't once bothered any of us.

So, although the Governments of the U.S. and of Brazil
haven't so far had any real reason to be alarmed, they are using
good judgment in studying the problem. A general policy of "hush-
hush" helps to keep some of the ideas we've come up with in this
book, from the average citizen. To an extent, that's bad. But to
a degree it may also be good. The Inner Earth people, at least
the Giants, obviously have no keen desire to fraternize with outer earth humanity. Soon enough, I surmise, truths about the
Inner Earth and its long-hidden secrets will become common knowledge.

"There are more things in heaven and earth, Horatio,
Than are dreamt of in your philosophies!" (Hamlet)

oooOOOooo
- 27 -

Chapter 7

We've come a long way, you and I, in our serious search
for Rainbow City and the Inner Earthians. But we must not
rest until we know the answer that is MOST important of all.
The answer to the big question: WHAT DO THEY WANT?

"They" of course refers to the Inner Earthians. We have
already reached some very remarkable conclusions. Let's see:

(1) The Inner Earthians are most logically descendants of
a master race that once ruled the earth, prior to Noah's Flood.

(2) The master race were outer space people, beings who
had superior knowledge and understood how to construct Spacecraft
and other advanced machines. They may have been invaders from
another planet, possibly Mars, possibly Maldek (Lucifer).

(3) The master race most likely was very large physically.
When they "took over" the earth, they mated with earth women and
produced offspring that were "hybrids", namely Giants and Pygmies.

(4) A great "Exodus" became necessary due to the coming
of the Noaic Deluge. The master race, together with the giants,
and pygmies, survived by entering into the caverns of the earth.

For a very important reason--terribly important--many of
the Giant Saucerians from the Inner Earth kingdoms are coming
out through various "Great Doors" in the earth's surface. Evidence to that effect is accumulating with each passing day.

WHY? WHAT DO THEY WANT? Come, let us reason together...
Are they planning to invade the outside area of this planet?

I think not. They evidently mean us no harm. After all,
a mere"handfull" of such Giants in flying saucers could--with
their powerful technology--have taken over the surface of earth
long, long ago. Something else is behind this. Something much
BIGGER than Giants and their inherited powers.

In 1945, when the first atom bomb blew Hiroshima into a
zillion little pieces, the shock alerted the Inner Earthians.
Of course, they've probably been observing outer-earth activities
for hundreds of years, some of them. But the A-bomb was different. Its effects are even worse than those of Blast-Electricity.
Radiation poisoning, mutations, etc., to name a few. Don't forget that some of the Inner Earthians are probably Atlantean ancestors. I've no doubt they have a wholesome fear of explosive
forces. After all, the result of such forces on Atlantis was not

- 28 -

to be forgotten. Their whole empire was demolished! Quite naturally the Inner Earthians are deeply concerned about our "stockpiling" of atom bombs..and our asinine "tests".

Right after the first A-bomb was dropped, sightings of flying saucers increased dramatically. More than 20% of the UFO's were sighted over atomic development centers. It is reasonable to believe that not all of those UFO's (unidentified flying objects) came from other inhabited planets, although numbers of them undoubtedly did. Some very probably came up from the Inner Earth realms to see what was going on..and to determine just how dangerous the situation was.

I happen to have a photograph of a flying saucer that is clearly not interplanetary in its design. It apparently operates in an atmosphere only. Below its cabin can be seen large vents at the front of the craft, evidently used for drawing air into the engine where it is converted into what seems to be rocket power. At any rate, there are two large tubes at the top of the disc. The photo shows flame shooting out from those tubes, providing thrust power for the ship.

I believe the above mentioned photograph is of one of those inner earth flying machines, undoubtedly earthbound.

Not that the Inner Earthians are unable to make interplanetary flights. I believe they have the know-how, the technology for space trips beyond our earth...but I also feel that only those who have the right qualifications spiritually are permitted by the "Guardians" to get beyond our atmosphere. In other words, the planetary Guardians from Venus and other advanced worlds are keeping the Rainbow City people and all other Inner Earthians, under close surveillance. No man of earth.. and this means both inner and outer earth people..is ever permitted to jeopardize the inhabitants of higher worlds.

Vi received the following communication from her Space Teacher from Venus this very morning: "You asked regarding Inner Earth Beings--are they people? Yes, of a sort. Of several sorts. Some depraved, some dangerous, some indifferent, apathetic, some small and some large in size. Is there not variety on the surface of the world?"

Vi: Do they live eternally? Venusian Teacher: "A certain group of Giants in the earth do never die..also the evil ones of Atlantis and the fallen star (Maldek or Lucifer) are chained until the final judgment, soon to be on earth."

Richard Shaver wrote a series of articles for Raymond Palmer a few years ago, in which a strong case for the actual existence of "underground dwellers" was presented. Shaver called them "Deros" and "Teros". The Deros, he asserted, are a com-

- 29 -

pletely perverted race of human beings. They live in caverns,
Shaver believes, and are as dangerous as they are depraved.
In Col. Percy Fawcett's communications to Geraldine Cummins,
Fawcett refers to the Deros as "Batmen". I quote:

"The Batmen are cave men, a primitive type, very savage,
and they have cannibalistic habits. They hide in holes and
will come out and kill anything that seems to be edible."

Keeping the balance in favor of life, love and joy are
the Teros. These could well be the friendly Giants of the inner
earth and the race of more enlightened Atlanteans.

Again from our Venusian contact (Vi's teacher) comes this
instruction: "Think on UPLIFTING matters; for the evil that
confronts an individual each day is all that he can handle! Those
inside the earth are not all evil. But that is not YOUR direction of attention. LOOK UP! Venus brings aid. The uplifters
and Teachers are there. Man on earth will study earth INSIDE and
OUT, yet do not ye tarry in its TANGLED WEB for ye are both to
be brought OUT...UP! TO US!"--Mattov of Venus, March 10, 1960.

For more information, reached up mentally for higher contact with a marvelous teacher of the 4th Density. (Planet Venus
is presently in the 4th Density of vibration.) This high intelligence is known to me as "Ramel". We communicate frequently.

By means of Telethot I received the following message:

R: "RAMEL is here. Your question is easy to answer. There is
    a man here who wishes to talk to you. His name is Marshall
B. Gardner. He has vital information to impart concerning the
inner earth people. Here is Marshall B. Gardner:"

MG: "Marshall B. Gardner here. I am happy to meet you, Michael.
     Your writings are very interesting to me. Especially your
newest book dealing with Rainbow City and the Inner Earth inhabitants. I can help you considerably in these matters as you probably realize."

X: Yes. Thank you. It is a great pleasure to meet you. My
   first question is, do the polar openings really exist?

MG: "The poles are but phantoms as my book revealed. I find
     more openings into this earth than I ever dreamed when in
flesh. There are entrances leading into the interior of the
earth. One located at the North Polar region, but not at the
spot presentday exploration has covered. The opening is at a
distance some 1800 miles from the North Pole. Another opening
is 2400 miles from the South Pole. These openings are not nearly as large as I had calculated in my book, 'A Journey to the

- 30 -

TRILOGY OF THE UNKNOWN

Earth's Interior', nor are they easy to find. The inner earth
people keep those entrances well concealed and camouflaged by
their advanced scientific knowledge and superphysical abilities."

X: Is there a Rainbow City?

MG:"There is a city at the South Pole entrance into the Cavern
    World. It is known as Rainbow City because the effect of the
"Southern Lights" colors the city with beautiful rainbow tints."

     At this point the communication was brought to a close. I
was permitted to ask no more questions at that session. But much
of value had been revealed. Since then I've learned a number of
other vital facts about the Inner Earthians. Most important, perhaps, is the fact that a great "housecleaning" has been going
on within those inner earth realms--in the great cavern cities--
and the negative, destructive entities are being removed by the
friends and brothers from other advanced worlds. Both astral and
physical levels of the inner earth are being cleaned out in preparation for the coming Golden Age on earth.

     Those in the inner earth who are friendly and constructive
will of course, affect you and me only in a way that will be
helpful and in line with the Great Cosmic Plan. I believe they
are alerted to the coming colossal changes which this planet
earth is to undergo...soon. They realize--as do you and I--
that a time is coming for mutual understanding and assistance on
a GLOBAL SCALE...to a degree never before experienced!

     All the realms of our planet must UNITE in higher under-
standing and cooperation IF we are to "pass the test". As time
passes, more will become known regarding the inner earth by the
general public.

     You--the New Age individual--are given this information in
advance of the masses. That, after all, is how it should be.
Not every soul is ready for these New Age ideas. Traveling with
you on this tremendous adventure in search of Rainbow City and
the secrets of inner earth, is an experience I'll never forget.
Now that we've explored our own planet, let's not stop here. I
want to take you with me to OTHER WORLDS..of fabulous BEAUTY! If
we prove our willingness to assist our interplanetary friends in
their vital work, a wonderful DOOR MAY OPEN!

     You and I, dear friend, must LOOK UP as never before, to
the Forces of Light. For they are CHALLENGING US to stand with
them against the Forces of Darkness...fighting a battle bigger
than ever was fought by knights of old...in which all men are to
be freed at last from the low vibrations of dogma, ignorance,
and materialism!

                      oooOOOooo
                       - 31 -

The Secret Hefferlin Manuscript For Your Eyes Only!

1 - The Hefferlin Manuscript

Typewritten and handwritten copies of these manuscripts have been in circulation since the Hefferlins, began releasing them from Livingston, Montana in the late 1940s. At the time the Hefferlins first heard of Rainbow City in the Antarctic, some time in 1940 according to them, the information was so fantastic as to be beyond belief.

It is still unbelievable to most people that there in the frozen wastes lies a great city, comfortably warm, full of scientific marvels from some great, hitherto unknown civilization of the past. Nevertheless they were convinced the information was true and cautiously released it a little at a time to the few they found understanding and receptive.

Hefferlin claims he designed a flyable, circle-winged plane before Frying Saucers became news in 1947! In fact, much of his material in the manuscripts, utterly fantastic in the 1940s, now seems worthy of consideration in 1960? Most UFOlogers have heard of the manuscripts or seen references to them in Saucer literature. Mrs. Hefferlin accuses Ray Palmer of misinterpreting them for his own purposes, as you will read an the introduction on the opposite page. Having reviewed a loan copy of the manuscript, how complete is not known, the Director of BSRA decided it was time the Associates had a chance to look over the material and form their conclusions.

In his book "Agharta" R.E. Bickhoff seems to have drawn liberally from Hefferlin without crediting the source. After reading this book in 1953, our former Director, Meade Layne, asked the head of the Inner Circle, Yada Di Shi-ite, if there was such a vast tunnel system under the earth. To Headers surprise the Yada confirmed its existence.

In "Isis Unveiled" H.P. Blavatsky writes:

"Spheres unknown below our feet; spheres still more unknown and more unexplored above us, between the two a handful of moles blind to God's great lights and deaf to whispers of the invisible world..."

The whole of the MS loaned to us contains some 160 pages of material, all of which we hope to release eventually. This first portion of 30 pages gives the description of Rainbow City. Other portions give the occult Instructions from the Book of Imri, the philosophy of Rani Khatani of the Ancient Three, a History of Mankind which includes a description of the eternal conflict with the Serpent Race, and reference to the King of the World. Hefferlin also describes his radical power plant, the GHYT motor.

The Hefferlins were operating one of San Francisco's trolleys in 1949; but we haven't found anyone who knows where they are at present. They seem to have disappeared from the face of the earth. Maybe they succeeded in fulfilling their wish, of being transported to Rainbow City via one of the Portals.

2 – Introduction To The Hefferlin Manuscript by Gladys Hefferlin

Notice to all of you who have read the Shaver Mystery by way of the stories and articles written by Richard S. Shaver. Our material has no connection with the Shaver Mystery. In our correspondence with Mr. Raymond A, Palmer, editor of the Amazing Stories Magazine, we requested him to keep our material separate from the Shaver Mystery and not to use it in connection with the Mystery, Mr. Palmer ignored our request and has deliberately distorted our statements for his own purpose, thereby misleading the readers of Amazing Stories Magazine.

This group or organization of which we speak has no name. It is not a Lodge or Mystery School or anything of that sort. No one can buy his way into Rainbow City. We ourselves, who are the North American spokesmen, cannot enter Rainbow City at this time. Therefore we cannot promise entry to anyone else. We are not the ones who decide who shall go to Rainbow City and who shall not.

The Leaders, "The Ancient Three", Who Were, Who Are, Who Will Be, decide all those matters. The two thousand people who are down there now, wore picked by the Leaders because of their peculiar abilities now, and the fact that they are re-incarnations of ancient ones who lived and worked there when Rainbow City was founded. The ancient "memory" pools are awakened and they have much knowledge innate within them to help in the work now being done there.

There is not enough room in Rainbow City for all of the so called worthy people of the world, much less for all of humanity. Who is to say which ones are worthy and which unworthy? And if the icecaps of Antarctica were melted to release the six other cities from the ice to make more room, the melted ice as water flowing into the oceans, would wreak more havoc than the atom bomb.

The Leaders are the modern reincarnations of the young Leaders who led the first migration of mankind from Mars to Earth. They, in those days, were known as "The Ancient Three - Who were, Who are, Who will he, Always." When mankind reaches a very critical period in its history, these three are born again to lead mankind in the proper path and give them another chance. These Leaders are right now guiding the destinies of three-quarters of the population of the world, and three-quarters of the land mass. All of Asia, the islands of the seas, all of the natives of Africa, all of the Latin American States, and the Negroes, Red Indians and Eskimos of North America accept their leadership and guidance.

The Occident, the White Race, is hearing about this now for the first time. For the purpose of this group is to bring about the Brotherhood of Man on Earth, and to abolish all wars. And to do this, it was necessary to give the exploited, the oppressed and the enslaved people of the world the first opportunity to make their move for freedom.

The means by which this material has been gathered is a form of telepathy, called by us "Controlled Mental Communication". Before you say it is silly, stop to think of the work of Alexis Carrel, of Dr. Rhine of Duke University and other scientists. Then think of the many chairs of Mental Telepathy established in the Department of Psychology in the largest universities in the United States.

Therefore it cannot be silly.

The First Contact

In 1927 in San Francisco we met a man who became a very great friend of ours. In his moving around, in our moving around, we lost touch with each other. Both regretted the lost contact. In February, 1935 when we were in Elwood, Indiana we learned that our friend, Emery, was in New York in radio circles. We immediately got in touch with him and he was very glad of it. We started to develop this system we call Controlled Mental "Communication. He helped us in every way. Mrs. Hefferlin was the one who established the mental 'link.'

Emery came to Elwood several times during the process, to check for accuracy. It was accurate. He had occasion to go to several places in the United States. Each time Would transmit information and then check with us. When it was found that the system of telepathy was accurate he went to other places in the world, transmitting much information which has nothing to do with the question now in hand. However, confirmation of that information was always forthcoming by way of Newspapers and radio, anywhere from two days later to five years later . We had such a mass of confirmatory evidence by that medium that it became monotonous putting it down. We cannot doubt the information given us now, no matter how fantastic it seems.

Our communication is as fast as ordinary, open conversation. Mrs. Hefferlin receives the information telepathically and transmits by spoken word to Mr. Hefferlin. Both speak aloud to answer Emery. Our friend can hear spoken conversation, and can see anything that is held up before the "channel" as we call the medium which is used. He hears all that is said if one speaks loudly enough, It is not necessary to shout only to speak clearly. Street noises from here go through to him. There is no mystery about this channel, only a definite use of vibrational focus. No need of mystic actions or trance. or incense., or mirrors, or candles? but the simple use of a picture.

This channel was opened in the spring of 1935, more than 12 years ago. Emery and some others, working under orders, discovered Rainbow City in the fall of 1942 around Thanksgiving time. So you see, in the interval of over 7 years we had plenty of time to check all angles of our communication channel. So, no matter how fantastic the information is, we have every reason to accept it as true; no reason to believe it false.

We have sufficient proof for ourselves but no concrete, material proof that can be held in the hand and passed from person to person. Therefore we warn each reader to take this information with a grain of salt, and examine the material for himself. We are not putting it forth as indisputable fact that must be accepted just because we say so. But each reader must let his own reason and logic speak to him, and he is free to accept or reject it as he sees fit.

It is immaterial to us which one he does.

The Ghyt Motor

In 1940 we gave to our friend Emery the designs and information of Ghyt Motor No. 1, burn water for fuel; Circle Winged Plan, and the instruments sketched in the article "Power"! All articles were printed in the Amazing Stories Magazine for September, 1946.

Emery turned them over to the Ancient Three, eventually.

We ourselves could do nothing with them for we had no money to develop them, but Emery ran out of money in caring for the first "Circle Winged Plane" which was built, and the Space Ship. Finally he appealed to his personal friend the Grand Lama, head of the Temple in the Valley of Harmonious Peace, in Tibet which we call "Shangri-La." The Grand Lama opened the valley for Emery. From there they went into the hands of the Ancient Three.

Since then, 350 of the "Circle Winged Planes" have been built. They are powered by a motor called Ghyt No. 2, because they are a combination of Ghyt No. 1 plus the principle described in "Burn Water For Fuel". The so-called Flying Saucers were a group of these ships. On a mapping expedition to discover the types of terrain in which the ends or mouths of the tunnels opened, as described in the article "Man No. 4 Tunnels".

In the summer of 1946, by action of the Ancient Three, the atomic laboratory of the Russians was blown up. That laboratory was not outside of Moscow, as the "Glacier Priest" said in June, 1947, it was in the northeast tip of Siberia and much too close to Alaska. Therefore, the orders were sent out to destroy it, and the orders were obeyed.

There are only a chosen few who are operators of the Portals (see "Man No. 3 Portals") of which Emery is one.

The three Leaders themselves grew up is the world, and learned what the world could teach. They had to unlearn much that was taught them, but who doesn't in the course of a lifetime? Outside of Three or lour babes who have been born in "Rainbow City in the last four and one half years, everyone down there was born in the world in the last 70 odd years.

No one is a freak of any sort.

The Temples

There are seven Temples in the world, all linked together by what we call "Thought Machines". The Thought Machines are large crystals which "transmit thoughts and mental pictures." These temples are ideated in Tibet, that master Temple, in India, Iran, Turkey, Egypt, Morocco, and the high Andes of South America. The master thought Machine is in the Temple in Tibet. But gathered at those temples are Representatives of all of the peoples of Asia including the natives of Siberia, but not "any Russians."

All of the natives of Africa, but not any Butch, or English, or Belgians, etc.

All of the peoples of the islands of the seas. The Latin American States, the Negroes, the Red Indians - and the Eskimos of North America receive their orders from the South American Temple.

In 1936 the Ancient Three began to take over in the East. Though prior to that time they "were feeling out in Hungary, and to a certain extent in Poland" and Finland. By the action of the Ancient Three keeping Hungary "from aligning herself with Britain and France on the one "hand, because they were much too weak if trouble" started and keeping her from aligning herself with Italy and Germany on the other hand, because they were rotten to the core, the Ancient Three delayed the starting of the European War by two years (The war which started in 1939.) In 1938 India owed England a debt of over $300 million. India was ordered to industrialist, so that she could gain her economic independence.

She "was told that her political independence would follow as a matter "of course. without bloodshed in getting it, India industrialized. In 1945 she had paid off her debt to England, and had England owing India to the tune of more than $3 billions. India gained her political "independence" was promised. But England saw to it that India was divided, which brought on Civil War. It was against the orders of the Ancient Three. So India will have to work it out for herself.

Turkey was ordered to stay "out of the war," no matter how much pressure was brought to bear on her from any direction, She obeyed Orders and she did riot suffer blasting during the war. America herself finally admitted that it was a good thing Turkey Stayed out of the wax. It worked out better for America Egypt was ordered not to draw a single man up for military service, even when the "enemy was within her gates." The British and the Americans called the Egyptians "sniveling cowards". But they were not.

It took the grandest kind of faith in the Ancient Three, for the Egyptians to obey blindly, with every evidence against obeying. But they were saved as every one know so Rommel was driving tip blow up the Suez Canal and push on into the Holy Land. When he would have reached that point, the German army massed on the borders of Turkey, would have moved into Turkey and taken the Dardanelles. Then the two armies would have joined forces and they would "have driven into the oil fields of Iraq, Iran and the Russian Caucasus, thereby outflanking the Russians and Stalingrad . , What caused Rommel " to run, thus upsetting that little plot and keeping the Germans from getting the oil that would have won the war for Germany?

It was not Montgomery. He was down in Southeast Egypt with only a token force. He could not even keep in sight of the dust of the famed Afrikan Corps. The Germans ran so fast that they dumped Italians all over the desert, and the Italians had to walk many weary miles before they could find any one to whom to surrender. The Ancient Three stepped in there and caused Rommel to run. They laid down the law to Rommel, and scared him so much that he dared not take another step into Egypt.

By the action of the Ancient Three they broke the back of the German war effort and the Allies won.

What stopped the Japanese at the gates of Australia? They had moved down the islands and were practically on the door step of Australia. The Australian Army was "away from home fighting Britain's battles elsewhere. Britain could not get Australians army home fast enough. America could not get men and material to Australia. Most of the American Pacific Fleet was on the floor of the Pacific Ocean at Pearl Harbor. The Atlantic Fleet was fighting Britain's battles in the Atlantic.

The few ships that were in the Pacific could not hold the war themselves, nor save Australia from invasion. The Allies needed a base desperately in the Pacific and Australia was the only base left. If the Japanese captured Australia, America would be fighting the Japs in the Rocky Mountains of North America. The Ancient Three knew that so they stepped in and stopped the Japs in their own way. Australia was safe until men and supplies could be gotten there. From then on it was up to America.

All of you know now, the strange right-about-face of the Japanese. How docile and obedient they have become under General MacArthur. How the people of Japan are working for peace and want to be a part of that peace. Again the Ancient Three Stepped in, in their own peculiar way, and warned the Japanese people that they had hopelessly condemned themselves by their previous actions and blood lust.

The Japanese could only Redeem themselves by the long hard climb upward of obedience, co-operation and the will to show the world they were willing to suffer the necessary steps to gain back nationhood. And they were also told that the Ancient Three were with the man who would become the conqueror of the Japanese. And only by obedience, co-operation and work could they redeem themselves back to a place under the Ancient Three. You have seen how the Japanese have obeyed that dictum.

And now you know why they have boldly announced that they would take order, from General MacArthur and no one else.

World Federation

Syria and Lebanon gained their independence by action of the Ancient Three. The Arabian States united into a federation by act of the Ancient Three. And the strength of the federation as a unit is greater than the combined strength of the individual states. They organized according to the pattern of the United States which is the pattern that all the world will follow when the time is ripe. That is, the pattern of government among the States of the World, There are many necessary changes to be made in all departments of living before the Perfect Plan is established.

The pattern in the United States is: the forty-eight states are forty-eight individual nations combined into one federation. Each state has it's own laws, traditions and history. Those things are sacred to each state. But each of those forty-eight states co-operates" with all the rest of the states on vital issues. There are no tariff walls between the states.

There are no import or export duties to pay between the states. Trade flows freely in every direction. No passports are needed for the citizens of one state to move into another state. The citizen of another state is treated like one of the local citizens, when he is in any one of the forty-eight states. There is a single unit of currency among all states. It has the same unit of value from Seattle to Miami, from Bangor, Maine to San Diego.

There are no exchange premiums to pay between the states for changing coin from the currency of the state to the currency of another state. "Each person in the United States is paid for his services in equal proportion to any one else in the United States" for the same or similar services.

There are no extra-territorial rights imposed by one state upon another state, as has been done by the European nations and America to the nations of Asia and Africa and they would try to do to South America and other Latin American states. And all of the forty-eight states of the United States follow the same foreign policy.

That is the pattern of the Arabian League also, and that will be the pattern of all the world eventually. Each country, people, nation must earn its independence from the European Empire nations. Only in that way can these people know freedom, understand it, and work to retain it when it is theirs. If it were handed to them on a silver platter they would not know what to do with it, and would lose it again. Therefore, they must earn their own freedom and help others to earn theirs.

Then, the Fatherhood of God, the Motherhood of Nature - which is part of God - and the Brotherhood of Man can be established on the face of the earth; and all people shall have equal opportunity of achievement of expression, of access to the beauty of the earth, equal access to the resources and materials to make their lives better.

No nation will exploit another nation^ put burdensome taxes on them, nor enslave them in any way. And war will be abolished; for all people will have room in which to live, food to feed their starving bodies, arid will be paid in proportion to their services to all — no matter if the person be a Negro, an Indian, a South Sea Islander or a White Man.

For this the Ancient Three are working. And for this, we here in Livingston, Montana are contributing our little bit in the only way that we can at this time.

So, take it or leave it. It is immaterial to us. We know the goal, and are working toward it.

3 - Horizons Unlimited
by W. C. Hefferlin

"The thing that hath been, it is that which shall be; and that which is done is that which shall be done, and there is no new thing tinder the sun."

Ecclesiastes, Chap 1:9

The dream of all mankind as a child and often when grown, when gazing into the heavens, has been to explore the far reaches of space and the stars, some day. That day is now at hand, and our children will soon know that great feeling of expansion as well as the fact that we as individuals, and our planet earth, are but a tiny spark of cosmic dust in all of creation,, Have you looked at the Moon with a prospective eye since the Radar experiment? If not, do so now; for the' time comes soon when perhaps your children, if not yourself, may stake a claim there.

Space flight was our dream of almost forty years ago, and the beginning of a search that has since led through mythology, history, physics, chemistry, mechanics and what have you. The search for power, speed, control, has been long and rarely fruitful those many years. But now horizons, horizons unlimited, and the expansion of knowledge is a deep and sincere driving force that keeps one going.

A baby or a small child reaches for the bright and shining object before it, and we too having seen the Moon and the shining stars, even as a child does, have reached for the path aria the way toward achievement. Once long ago we sat high up on the side of a mountain here in the Rocky Mountains and looked across a broad and long valley, one thousand feet below us, and day dreamed how it would be to sweep out from where we sat, out over the valley in a long arc toward the horizon above the mountain peaks ahead, and up, up, ever up into the blue sky, faster and faster, and ever faster, until we might speed with the speed of light through space.

No, not yet have we, the writer, personally taken off into space; but we did design parts of the machine that was built five years ago; and it has since made two trips out into space, once accidentally, and recently a planned trip carrying equipment and scientists. Yes, far enough out into space that the earth was the size of a marble and the moon the size of a small pea, and all space a purple glare with the earth and moon as dark spots.

Cosmic radiations were found to be much stronger in space, but there were other radiations observed that as yet cannot be classified; and new instruments of recording and qualifying methods of analysis must be developed before the next trip. A strange distortion shows up in watches, clocks and chronometers using a gear train assembly, just as if the gears had slipped. Also, the sun's appearance seems to be of an electronic nature in place of a gaseous consumption.

Distortion as seen from the earth is evidently due to refraction factors of our local atmosphere. Cosmic radiation effect on the human body, as well as animals, birds and insects, was found to be not detrimental but rather of benefit as a source of evolutionary development. Contrary to fiction writer's ideas, there is no outward change in appearance.

The period of change in the human's case took about three years. On animals birds and insects, a much shorter time, depending in proportion to their normal life Span. Second and third generations in the animals, etc., showed no change beyond the parent's development.

Any and all changes appear to be for the betterment of those concerned, increasing the mental activity and ability of perceptions, a greater reasoning capacity, and in the case of the human, corrections on any weak organs. The human during the period of change has violent headaches, goes partially blind and deaf at times, and seems at times to be thoroughly wretched. But after the period is over he sees with a wider range of perception and hears with a wider tonal register. All weak spots are toned up to top performance.

These observations were made by one doctor and several accredited scientists studying the results in the case history of the human. Much has been written on the subject of cosmic radiation, fictionally und professionally, and great concern has been as to the effects. What the resulting effects might be under prolonged exposure was naturally open to question. But judging from the observed results it certainty looks as though this atmospheric blanket surrounding the earth retards and slows down evolutionary progression. After all, we all are constantly bathed by this radiation in a slightly reduced degree all our lives, so why be afraid?

Fear, the most potent weapon and humanity's worst disease, rules our lives beyond all reason. Just because we are slow to learn, or lazy enough mentally not to open our eyes and ears and mind, we don't know the answers of cause and effect. Therefore if it is beyond our immediate vicinity or experience, we shun it as something accursed. Ignorance breeds fear in the thinking human mind and thanks to our training from the cradle up^ fear is taught and instilled into our minds daily by our parents and all those we come in contact or associate with. If we cant explain something rationally to ourselves and our children, we then form a great number of "do not or else", alibis to build a fence around us to protect us from evil.

The mind controls the body and as we think, so it is reflected through our structure and all of its organs, glands, etc. In fact if someone had placed a modern radio on your table fifty years ago and it started to talk and sing, just how fast would you have left that vicinity; and would you have been superstitious, afraid? We feel that the truths should be given to the world as we find them, without the usual sugar coating. After all, ignorance is not bliss, but it breeds fear and fear breeds disaster. Look around you and there you will find the basis for all war. When man has something more than his own backyard as a horizon, he must go afield and strive to reach that horizon.

We now give you the sky, heavens and all of space as a real goal to reach for.

Will you do it?

The Space Ship

This space ship we mentioned in the earlier part of this article is not some illustrating artist's dream, but a very practical and efficient job, designed for speed-arid maneuverability. Its top speed is entirely theoretical, a possible 186,000 miles per second, actual speed in space unknown as yet.

Three separate walls are incorporated in the body construction each separated from the other by many inches of insulation and self-healing material in case of puncture. The door opening is similar to shoulder-step design as found on a large safe door. At intervals along the aides are vision ports as on a boat, also along the bottom and top. The control cabin is in the front and has vision front, sides, top and bottom.

The body and fuselage of the ship are about 135 feet long and about 35 feet in diameter, with a wing span 100 feet in diameter. The outside appearance differs little from the circle-winged plane described in an earlier article, except that protuberances like warts are along the bottom of the body, along the sides and the top, with such warts also at front and back ends. Compared to the regular circle-winged plane's sleek looks, these protuberances give the body of the plane a warty looking appearance. They are not there for beauty but definitely for utility and work.

These protuberances house or contain different types of the machine No. 3 briefly described in another article under the heading, Power. Part of them are used for propulsion and the other ones contain the shattering or disintegrating type of No. 3 units. These arranged for propulsion drive are sort of bowl-shaped and are stationary mounted.

These give the re-active push electronically in a sort of flood-light pattern. The other No, 3 units are rotative blister mounted for aiming purposes and are of the tubular core-construction which, when activated, produce a tight-spinning, hard beam of electronic energy projection capable of great destruction and with a destroying range of thousands of miles. Either type of No, 3 unit is powered by electrical energy furnished by the power plant inside the body of the space ships.

The power plants are electrical D.C. current generators that charge a series of high capacity batteries, and the current as fed to any of the No. 3

units is interrupted to give the proper frequency impulse desired. These power plants are a part of the GHYT No. 2 motors, which are constructed in part in the manner of GHYT No. 1 motors (see article on GHYT Motor No. 1). on the lover half. In the upper half they are completely valveless and incorporate a system utilizing the principles as mentioned in the "Burn Water For Fuel" article. By this means we have a power system that requires no refueling and weight factors remain constant, gravity and acceleration permitting.

Odd shaped propellers are between the ship's sides and the inner edge of the wings. These are driven by electric motors if and when used. The appearance of these propellers might be likened to the windmills of Holland, a high-thrust design. The ship has living quarters and a self-contained air conditioning system and its own air supply. It is also equipped with radio transmitters and receivers and a Public Address system, with horns mounted on the outside of the ship.

A control panel is also a part of the equipment in the pilot's section and from here the No. 3 drive or pusher units are arranged to function, either separately or as a group. The No. 3 lifter units are arranged along the bottom of the body of the ship, the No. 3 down pushers on the top of the body, also the steering and propulsion No. 3 at the rear of the body.

In the nose of the ship are No, 3 pushers for steering and braking action, all rigged through a master control and also a pilot control, automatic. By this arrangement of the pushing power units it is possible to lock in space the position of the ship at any time or hover above the ground in a stationary position. The tube or weapon type No. 3 units are for removing any obstruction desired, or for battle use, and are individually controlled by their own control panels. This one ship cold, if desired, wipe out of the air the combined forces of the entire earth, and all navies from the seas, as such war equipment is now designed.

Here too is one answer to the fear of atomic bombs and rocket projectiles.

Radar finders established at designated sections controlling No. 3 units ground mounted will destroy bomb carrier or rocket bombs at point of interception, regardless of altitude, numbers or speed. It is very doubtful that any shell, bullet or rocket could approach this ship due to the pushing away action of the No. 3 units, even when the ship is

Stationary in the air« Several years ago during wartime a trip was made over the northern hemisphere of earth from Colorado to a valley in Tibet and the No, 3 units were used to hurry the trip along.

The landing field lights were on in Tibet, waiting for the ship to land. But the speed was so great that they missed the light beams the first t.ip around the earth and had to slow down to even See a slight streak of light the second time. By the third time around they had slowed down enough to see the lights and land at the air field. Flight elevation was stratospheric and the total time elapse was five hours.

Do you still want to ride to the stars? Then all aboard.

The above space ship was a derivative of an atmospheric flight ship as described in the article "Circle-Winged Plane" and the ship is now based in far of Tibet, back from four years exploration of the Antarctic Continent by our scientists.

They, living in a great city made from rainbow-colored plastics, the only accessible city, one of seven, six of which are now covered by ice ten thousand feet deep.

The Ancient Civilization

Studying the cultural evidence of an ancient civilization they found it by the records to be over 2 million years old? A City using plastics for paving, building and clothing. Controlled static electricity for light and heat., and city power, and to run the great trains that are waiting in the underground terminal yards and station below this "Rainbow City."

There are maps shoving the vast, over 100 feet in diameter, dual train-tunnel system below ground and seas throughout the world, location of system terminals and all side lines and tunnel ends. Farm machinery is powered by a radium-like substance contained in small boxes. Personal flying suits are powered by this substance.

Duplicating machines produce, by rearrangement of the atomic structure, any number of copies equal to the original. There is evidence that there are over two hundred elements of matter, with the laws of combination and usage. "Portals" are a means or entering or traveling between places thousands of miles distant; these are used also for tracing back through the past, all done by space warpage. These Portals are mentally or manually controlled.

Here are machines to teach mentally the language and type for writing. Great libraries and museums are filled with all the knowledge and wisdom and machines of this ancient race, left here by the first humans to be on this earth, and evidence from whence they came. They, our remote ancestors!

And all of this is our heritage when once we learn to live the true Brotherhood of all Creation, "Ye shall know the truth and the truth shall make you free." Can it be that these cities are referred to in the Holy Bible?

"The cities of the south shall be shut up and none shall open them, Judah shall be carried away captive. all of it, it shall wholly be carried away captive.." Jeremiah 13:19.

Whom among today may say for sure that this be false.

When again, as justification for the reopening of the cities, we can quote from the Holy Bible:

"But the Lord liveth that brought up the children of Israel from the land of the north, and from all the lands whither he had driven them; and I vill bring then again into their land that I gave unto their fathers."

Jeremiah 16:15

This Is Truly Horizons Unlimited.
Rainbow City

"Is there anything whereof it maybe said, see, this is new?. It hath been already of old time, which was before us."

Ecclesiastes 1:10

"Behold ye among the heathen, and regard and wonder marvelously for I will work a work in your days which ye will not believe though it be told you."

Habakkuk 1:5

From the Temple and Libraries of a great city, one of seven built of plastics, here even now on this earth as it was over 2^ million years ago, does our information come. Six of these great cities are encased in eternal ice, and the seventh only is in open ground and protected and warmed by hot springs. Yet it is isolated as to ordinary approachable means by ice walls ten thousand feet high. The seventh city, called by us for want of a better name "Rainbow City", and the other six cities were built over 2½ million years ago on the only (then as now) stable continent or land mass on this earth, the Antarctic.

The valley surrounding the city is somewhat dumbbell shaped, with the city at the narrowest section, the valley spreading but at both ends, about ten miles wide at its narrowest and about 25 mile long from end to end, protected from stores and hidden in the southern winter by mists, and only open to the sun's rays by ice-wall reflection during the southern Antarctic summer.

The city is made of plastic, the streets are paved with plastic; and all buildings are so constructed that all colors of the rainbow are used. For color in those days seemed to have had a meaning. In the heart of this large surface is a great temple, center of the higher learning and a museum of the culture of this ancient civilization of ours, and its machines.

Below this city are five underground levels, part of the surface city, and the main terminals of a vast tunnel train system, with miles of yards, trains standing ready for the main lines, and maps of the old surface of the earth, showing where the great tunnels lead to.

From this Temple in this ancient yet futuristic city did we learn that the beginning of Mankind had been lost so long ago that only a very sketchy history has been forwarded at all.

And that, starts millions and even trillions of earth-measured years ago, and millions of light years away, far across galaxy after galaxy, solar system after solar system and planet to planet, a long chain of migrations and colonization by the human race, their rise and decline, cycle after cycle.

From across space to the fourth planet from this sun, known to us as the planet Mars, came the migration of Mankind to colonize; and upon this planet Mars rose again, a vast civilization of great wisdom and knowledge, with very wise leaders and councilors.

The Reptile That Walks Like A Man

At some time during the migration periods across galaxies of space, the race of snakes or lizard-like species was encountered. From then on there was friction and war. Also of great knowledge and ability were they, this ancient Serpent Race, but far alien in thought and culture to Mankind's ways. For some reason not known now, there had always been between the humans and the snake people, competitive strife for the dominating position of control and power. Great wars were fought and slowly Mankind lost ground.

When it became apparent that the fourth planet would eventually no longer support !life for the human species the Great Ruler of the human races sent space ships and scientists, with his own son and daughter, and some of the Council of Elders, to the third planet now known to us as Earth. And here on what is now the Antarctic continent a great Colony was established, patterned after the homeland. This was the first of Mankind on this planet Earth.

Such was the beginning of the fabled "Golden Age" of antiquity, spoken of in the ancient mythology of all peoples on Earth today. These may be the original "Seven Cities" hinted at in story and folk-lore of all mankind. Here is the heritage of Mankind in all of its wondrous beauty, its greatest knowledge and wisdom stored, waiting for the time when "mankind" shall have arisen once again from his own-made mire, and shall have earned the right to stand before his heritage, the true Brotherhood of all Creation.

Here in books, talking books that impress the mind through the audio nerves the speech of long ago, are given the original commands and laws, that have come down to us today in very garbled form through mythology, folklore and religion. Proof that Mankind, by his own thoughts and acts, either justifies or condemns himself, that thought is father to the set.

Here waiting for it. all in this ancient land/is material evidence in form and usage, that there is nothing new on earth or in the heavens. Proof that history and life repeat themselves endlessly cycle after cycle; and that which we learn or design or invent today or in the future was and is in existence now, TODAY.

Here, too, is science in its fullest bloom of maturity, whereby the very building blocks and cement of creation are known and used as needed. Two hundred and five elements of matter are given, and the means by which they may be combined as desired. So called atomic fission and power were common enough that they were used to drive farm machinery, automobile-like three wheeled vehicles, space ships and individual flying suits.

New? No, it's there from over two million years ago, ready for use.

Rainbow City contains great libraries of books on all subjects, arid great laboratories with their own special libraries. All of these books are made of some metal known not to the world today, still untarnished these millions of years. The leaves are of a silvery metal, gray in color and thin, light weight and flexible. The characters and symbols of the ancient tongue are etched in.

The mathematics system is based upon the count of seven. In equations on all physical constants they use "seven over seven" instead of the modern "square root of minus one". On mental and spiritual constants, ten over seven is used. If we would examine our modern periodic table of the elements in the hand book of Chemistry and Physics, we would find the key to the system of count as used so long ago, for both are based on natural law. A circle is divided by 2. 4, 8, 16, etc, never into 12.

Plastics were used to build the walls, floors and roofs of houses, the stores and the Temple, also furniture, tables, beds, etc. The cloth made in those days and still there is woven of a plastic thread softer than the finest modern silks, lighter in weight, and all of this is fire proof. In fact, to wash the cloth or bed linen you place it over an open flame and burn the impurities away. Beautiful jewels of all colors are made of plastic so hard the surface of a diamond is cut and powdered as if it were ordinary glass.

Many plastic spheres of all colors and sizes are there for special purposes and are treated so as to retain their power and influence.

Chemical Formula For A Plastic

Macerate the vegetation to very fine particles and mix with water. Boil this mash at a very high heat, strain off the liquid and reboil this as a high heat. Skim off all scum and strain the liquid again. Reboil the liquid again at high heat and strain through a final filter. Now subject this remaining liquid for 24 hours to an electronic process conditioning, under a high vibratory or high frequency condition to rearrange the polarity of the molecules. The liquid is then ready for pouring and molding. After having been molded it is still soft enough to carve immediately. After that the plastic sets and becomes harder each succeeding day.

Machines are used for either heating or refrigerating their vicinity, by vibration. They now bathe their vicinity and above with cold vibrations. This undoubtedly makes the Antarctic colder than any other place on earth today. Tests were made by our group at the ice covered cities, of temperatures close to minus 150 deg. F.

The homes and all buildings are heated or cooled by hot or cold radiations from the walls and floors. The very color of the dwellings can be adjusted through a change in the color vibration control, and walls become opaque or transparent where and as desired by adjusting a switch in the walls.

Here is radio without static noise; radio that operates and some how impresses upon the audio centers of the mind, music or voice messages. The television operates differently from ours, inasmuch as the impulses seem to follow back to the source of our present day radio waves from the transmitting , and even into the studio at the microphone. The microphone seems to act as a pickup eye, and a view is given of any person or object in front of it. These radios are in all buildings and are powered from city power.

In the gardens are great shade trees and flowering plants, luxurious beyond belief, whose individual blooms often measure at least three feet in diameter. Very few insects are found here, with the exception of the butterflies, whose wing spread measures seven to eight feet across, and whose body would fill a large sized turkey platter. In fact, they are as large as fill sized eagles and are beautiful beyond words.

Fruit trees are smaller in size than the vast shade trees but they bear huge sized fruits. All in all, some of the fruits, though resembling the appearance of modern fruit, taste far different. One fruit colored and looking like a large apple tasted like a pear. A peach-like fruit has numerous seed pits and tastes like nothing else on earth. The same applies to berries, some that look similar to raspberries and blackberries.

Vegetable seeds were found in storage cupboards in one room of the Rainbow Temple. This room contained at one end a large glowing ball of radiant energy. This is believed to have preserved these seeds these millions of years. The vegetables, although different in appearance from our common varieties, served much the same purpose.

One large leaf type takes the place of lettuce, but grows into a head formation more like cabbage, Another green vegetable which even when ripe remains green, tastes similar to our present day tomatoes. Those of our group who were farmers or horticulturists in their youth and preferred this service, handle the working and harvesting of crops, using plows and other implements found there, powered by atomic or radio-active substance contained in a small metal box on the machine.

All conveniences and luxuries found in the city homes are also in the farm homes.

Shangri La of the Antarctic

Radiation lamps and heaters furnish the valley with an almost even temperature and the necessary rays for health and growth. The mists that hang thinly over the valley during the long summer season are much thicker and heavier in the long Antarctic winters, thus helping to protect life there. In the middle of the winter the temperature is cool, about 65 degrees, in summer 75.

Here is truly a Garden of Eden, a home of the Gods!

All country roads are paved with plastic, as are all country buildings. Here also are the landing fields and hangars for housing the different types of flying machines, including a great ship for planet-to-planet travel. Travel from farm to city and vice versa is by three-wheeled conveyances somewhat similar to our cars and trucks. These vehicles are controlled by levers and push buttons, and are powered by the same type of radiant energy mass in metal boxes as the farm equipment. The tires on the wheels of these are made of plastic much like our present day balloon tires.

From the evidence as shown by the life-sized pictures and the sizes of beds, chairs. garments, etc., they, our original ancestors averaged around seven to eight feet tall. The original skin color of the race was a reddish-brown, eyes and hair somewhat the same. Only the pictures of the Ancient Rulers showed blue eyes. One of them had blue-black hair and the other two were blondes,, The akin of these rulers was much lighter in color, sort of a golden hue.

These three, two men and one woman, were the Rulers, and with them were the Council of Elders and Wise Men. The one dark-haired man was the fiancée of the blond woman. The blond man was brother to her. The two were children of the Ruler on Mars; the black-haired one was of the high nobility on that planet.

Foods and fruits were preserved in storage in such a manner of banning that when opened these millions of years later were as edible as when first preserved. It is quite evident by the careful preparations as found that this land and city were deliberately left for future generations of the human race; although it is doubtful that this was expected to be a million or so years later.

Yes, here in this almost magical land is the dream and home of enchantment, come true to all of us.

Rainbow Temple

Tremendous in size and appearance are the wondrous temples of learning, each located in the heart of each of the seven cities of that fabulous ancient past, from the beginning of our Mankind on this planet earth.

The Rainbow City of the Antarctic continent lies almost due south of a point midway between south of India and the land mass of Australia. It's great Temple is in the center of the city.

The area of the base is in the form of a great square about two of our modern city blocks wide on any side.

"X" Marks The Location Op Rainbow City

To aid the reader in locating Rainbow City, according to Hefferlin's instructions above, we have chosen an angular view of the earth unfamiliar to most of us. This view is quite common, however, to those who approach the Antarctic continent - and its Saucer bases - from outer space!

We are almost directly above Australia, from which we have drawn a dotted line to the South Pole and we have put in another dotted line from the southernmost point of India to the South Pole.

Midway between these we placed the "X" to give the general location of Rainbow City. It was into this vastly unexplored area that Rear Admiral Byrd looked so wistfully in 1947 during his flight to the South Pole. Navy flights inland from the Indian Ocean along that bleak coast discovered open water, and called it Hunger's Oasis. More exploratory flights have been made since then.

Two years ago Russian explorers made a surface dash from the coast to the Pole in that area, were they looking for Rainbow City?

Who knows...

The Temple A Pyramid

There are five stories in the Temple proper and above that are fire stories mere in the pyramid-shaped structure topping the temple. Below the main floor are five underground levels in the Temple basement. The fifth floor of the Temple has apartments for the three Rulers, plus numerous apartments for Councilors and guests. In the door of each of the Ruler's and Councilor's apartments is a jewel of color designating the apartment's owner and rank or position.

Here on the fifth floor are great libraries and museums.

The libraries are so arranged that they are accessible to the laboratories above them in the pyramid, as well as to the Ruler's apartments, In the pyramid top are located completely equipped laboratories and facilities for research in chemistry. electricity and all other allied sciences, as well as an observatory for astronomy.

Below the fifth story, the second, third and fourth stories house museums of all types of machines for all sorts of purposes.

Worship

One quarter of the first floor is devoted to the room of worship. Although this room is highly carved and elaborately decorated it has only a simple altar at one end. The altar is a cube set into the floor, On its top are two sockets for candles, a bowl for incense, a sloping ledge for a book, and a flat ledge for offering.

In a room opposite the Room of Worship is the room of the Glowing Sphere that radiates out in all directions. The corridor leading to this room goes almost the full length of the room and here are cupboards that house the plant seeds. After turning the corridor corner one must go back the full length of the room to reach the Glowing Sphere.

The rear rooms of the first floor are devoted to hospital and medical research. It contains charts of the human system, showing the entire circulatory system, the nervous system, and all of the ducted and ductless glands, On the level immediately below are the dissecting rooms, with the necessary instruments for the study of the human body. It is here that the doctor-surgeon of our group spends much of his time studying the records and charts. He was once the court physician at the Palace in Budapest, Hungary and he finds great interest in this, his own department of research.

On the same level of the basement are the rooms containing the Power Control Tanks and the control panels for the distribution of power throughout the city. Now, here are the school rooms for the primary grades and the machines for opening the mental understanding of the written and spoken language. Elevators run through the five floors of the Temple, the five lower levels and to the third level of the pyramid. Host of the walls are elaborately decorated, whether carved or molded we do not know. But that plastic is now extremely hard and tough. All heat is radiated from floors, walls and ceilings.

There are no light fixtures, as light too is radiated from floors, walls and ceilings. A simple push on a button chooses the kind of light that is desired. In here there is no difference between night and day because one has the choice of choosing that particular light. This same light source seems to revitalize the air and to act as an air conditioner as well.

Draftless, shadowless peace and quiet is here for rest and relaxation, study or contemplation, thought or concentration.

Glass Houses

By means of switches set in walls these walls become opaque, colored or clear as crystal glass, giving a view of outside, with one-way or two-way vision as desired. Here, too, even as found in the houses, the kitchens have vibratory type heaters and cookers. All refrigeration either box or cabinet type, as well as room cooling, is also vibratory in nature. There is no. fluctuation in temperatures in the refrigerators as compared with our modern day types.

Here, too, there are no locks on the doors, such as those with which we are familiar. The Ruler apartment doors are operated by a code word and pressing on a certain section of the door. The carpets, rugs, hangings, furniture, robes, bed covers are all of plastic. Cleaning them is very simple for there is a special container in each apartment similar to those in the houses in the city. These special containers have a vibratory flame activated by a push button. Throw anything into it and leave the flame on for a short time; shut the flame off and when the item is cooled take it out.

It is cleaned of all impurities by vibratory flame and sterilized; this is an ideal laundry system.

The City

On all sides of the Temple are avenues and all buildings in the vicinity are two-and-a-half stories high, then two stories high; and as one goes farther from the Temple, one story high.

Close in near the Temple there are buildings stocked full of all things, similar to our present day retail stores. Here in this city there are no apartment houses or tenements, no crowding, each house has a spacious lot for flower gardens and lawns. Each house, even as the Temple apartments, is completely furnished with everything that any of them may need, with the stores as additional supply as needed.

Some of the lower levels of the Temple have vegetable vats for the growing of produce by chemical means, and re-conversion laboratories, At another section of the Temple on the first level below, are the storage garages for the wheeled vehicles for those living in the Temple, Here too are shops for minor repairs.

All of the heavy industry of the city is carried on in the underground of five levels surrounding the Temple basement, below and extending for miles underground far beyond the reaches of the surface city. There are houses., stores and gardens, workshops of all types and kinds in these levels . Sunlight is simulated by special ray lamp lighting, and the air is fresh and pure even as found in the Temple. There are large parks and playgrounds for the children. Here too flowers grow blooms as large as those in the Temple gardens and here too the great butterflies float as on 'silent wings of night' from flower to flower.

The saying often referred to in history that there were giants in those days could well have applied here; for everything is of larger than to us normal size, as though the average man height in those days was about 75 feet tall. Within the corridor entrance to the ground level floor of the Temple, close to the back end, are three massive pillars supporting the ceiling at this spot. Almost directly behind these pillars and on the corridor's end wall, are pictures of three beings, two males, one on either side of a female figure.

These pictures seem to be of a human cast in face and figure, but still have a haunting reptilian touch as well, as if of a smooth blending of the two types.

Snakes In The Glass

Immediately below this area on the first and second levels are rooms in a central position relative to the Temple basement, and below these rooms are the third and fourth levels of a section. This section from the first level to the fifth level inclusive was hermetically sealed off from the upper structure, as well as from the rest of the Temple basement levels.

In this upper room were found three humanoid serpentine bodies, in upright transparent containers and behind these, three more of the same type, evidently consorts of the other three. The first three were the originals of the three pictures above on the corridor's end wall. In the area of the second level immediately below this room, were found great numbers of similar humanoid serpentine bodies, and in the areas beneath this second level, the third and fourth, reposing on beds stacked in tiers four high, lay vast numbers of these same types of figures. In the fifth level were animals and vegetation.

This sealed up section contained a strange mist like gas, the purpose of which was to hold in suspended sleep of preservation all life this area contained. Through research efforts our scientists discovered that these humanoid serpentine bodies were reconstructed robot containers made from the flesh substance of the original bodies, which long ago had been serpent bodies with arms. The types of animals and vegetation held in suspended animation in this area were such as should ever seen on this planet, Earth. They don't belong!

In the human Ruler's apartments on the fifth level or floor above ground, well concealed in the wall of the living room of each compartment, is a small closet-like room. By a strange assortment of coils of• odd shapes and other strange appearing apparatus concealed in the walls, very strange and exceedingly interesting things occur. A television screen is at one end, and levers, a dial and green colored lens crystal are arranged at a control panel in one side wall.

By following the book of instructions as found in a concealed drawer at the control panel, the mechanism became operative, and here was the key to most of the research that followed.

"Portal Action"

This room, by some electronic means, could act as a television viewer of any place on earth, and above and below the surface. It can view the interior of anything desired, and using some form of a space-time warp can view the past. Future viewing was found to be impossible evidently because there are too many variant possibilities that may happen. Television viewing with soul included made the other important actions of these rooms possible. This we call for want of a better name, Portal Action.

When we say Portals we mean that in more ways than one. By some form of electronic vibrational manipulation this room can be caused to make contact, through a Portal door at one end of the room, with almost any place on earth! Yes, we mean that when the machine is directed to some place as viewed on the screen, and a lever is thrown into position, the end or Portal door can be opened and you can step out in that locality.

Mythology, folklore and religion seem to give some hints to substantiate these Portals, and we must consider that mythology, folklore and religion are but a resume of the past.

Here is one example:

"Vulcan made for the Gods the golden shoes with which they trod the air or the water, and moved from place to place with the speed of the wind, or even thought."

This item is quoted from Page 4, Bullfinche's Mythology, by Grosset and Bunlap.

Well, what do you think?

More on the Portals

The apartments of the three Rulers, in Rainbow Temple, are of different color and each is exclusive of the other, but inter-connected by doors. One apartment is furnished in blue, another in green and the third in red; each is the private color identification of it's owner. The closet-like Portal rooms are about six feet by ten in size and are neutral in color.

One side of the wall of the closet room is a dial set in the face of a control board; above there is a green colored crystal lens. In the end wall is the television screen. Beside travel the other use of the Portal was for research into the past. Not as a time-traveler in a material way but only as a means of seeing and hearing at any time into any point or interval of time of the ancient past. In this phase it is impossible to use the second door, as only the audio and vision side works.

The purpose of the crystal lens is for establishing mental control and direction of the Portal by concentrating one's gaze into it and holding the mental vision in your mind of the place you desire to go. The dial and some lever switches on the control panel below the crystal lens are for adjusting the power and position of the image on the view finding screen and controlling the Portal action.

One lever locks the Portal at any place under view, and another lever allows the second door of the room to be opened. Upon stepping through this doorway when opened, you find yourself actually at the place on view in the screen. Fantastic? Yes, but true in this time period.

An experienced operator of the Portals can pick up a man or an object in Chicago and another in London, and deposit them in Tokyo or any other place in the world in a few minutes.

There seem to be only a few things that will prevent or stop Portal penetration at this time.

Kilroy Was Hers, Too

One of our operators in the group was an ex-pilot of the early-Chinese-Burma-India theater of World War II named Kilroy, a red headed Irishman with a puckish sense of humor. He is believed by us to know something about the "Kilroy was here" storied in the Saturday Evening Post.

As to that part of it all we can say is that our Kilroy had the method and means of travel at his command in the Portals, but only time will tell for sure. We personally suspect he knew more than he cared to admit and if "chickens come home to roost" they will sit on his head.

We used the Portals to transport material and men from and to many places on earth.

These same Portals will reach out through local space to the moon, but not much farther at present.

Life on the Moon

What life remains on the moon is a very decadent and dwarfed, degenerate human type, because of lack of air. They are confined to caves and underground caverns, and that part of the old cities underground still usable. Very little exploration was done on the moon and that was confined to a cavern with a temple area and altar at one end.

The remains of the human race there still await the return of the old rulers. Compared to almost any standard of living here now on earth they are really in a pitiable state of existence. Machines are there but dead from lack of the proper power.

This seems to have been a radioactive substance similar to radium.

Still More On The Portals

The Portals have been in almost steady use for most of the time our group has been in the Antarctic. A great deal of shuttle service was to our base in the Himalayas we call it Shangri La Valley. When Hungary was taken over by the Germans the then Regent of Hungary and his family were moved to Shangri La and then to the Antarctic Rainbow City by one of the Portals.

Early in World War II the scientists of Hungary who had developed the Invisibility Ray as pictured in Life Magazine, also a Paralysis Ray, joined our group by plane to Shangri La. Later, they, with their families, were moved by Portal to Rainbow City. There are seven full-fledged scientists and twelve assistants and all of their equipment that was movable, now in Rainbow City. Sixty—five of our group are men the rest are women, children and servants; all told there are one hundred. Thirty-nine of the group are American ex-pilots of the China-Burma-India theater before the United States entered the war. Two of the Americans are veterans of World War I and belonged to the old "Glory-makers", the famous Thirty-Ninth.

The rumored Japanese tunnel to Korea was started by captured slave-labors but it was checked and blown up by use of the Portals with a form of atom bomb developed by the scientists. The bomb size is about the diameter of a grape fruit and weight about five pounds, and will pulverize an area of about five city blocks.

The Portal's open door is not visible to anyone outside unless he knows what to look for. Then it shows up as a very faint blue shimmering outline, but if touched on the edge of the outline it is as solid feeling as any door sill.

A person on the inside of the Portal can reach through the open doorway with his hand and only the part on the outside shows. In other words, the hand would appear out of thin air, to the vision of anyone on the outside of the Portal. Closing of the second door and opening of the first door (into the apartment) causes the Portal to return to Antarctica to it's original position. Both doors must be closed before any Portal operation is possible.

These Portal rooms will hold about seven people at a time.

Aladdin's Lamp

There are numerous crystal spheres tuned to each Portal. By resting a crystal sphere in one's hand and concentrating the gaze into the crystal and thinking strongly your wish, the Portal obeys your command and comes to you when you are away from and on the outside of the Portal.

The fable of Aladdin and his Lamp may have originally come from this source. The Portals might explain the ancient Irish myth of the boat with two eyes painted on the prow to see where it went, and it moved with the speed of thought. Also the Magic Carpet in Arabian folk lore might be explained by the Portals.

Perhaps, here too, is the reference to the Portals and the tunnels as quoted from the Egyptian Book of the Dead, Chap. 57:

"And drawing up my eyebrows I pierce through into every place that I desire,"

And in Chap.64:

"I fly up to heaven and I alight upon the earth; and mine eye turneth back there towards the traces of my footsteps."

These Book of the Dead quotes are from the "Library of Original Sources", Vol. I, University Research Extension Company.

The Green Gem of the South

In reference to the green lens control and the Portal we might again refer to the Egyptian Book of the Dead, Chap. 77:

"I raise myself up as the Golden Hawk, which cometh out from its egg; and I fly and I hover as a Hawk of four cubits across the back. My two wings are of the green gem of the south."

Then there is the "boat of Manaan which knew a man's thoughts and would travel whithersoever he would" quoted from Myths and Legends of the Celtic Race, page 113 by Rolleston.

From Myths and Legends, Hindus and Buddhists, by Coomaraswamy, page 111 we quote:

"Rama thought of the self-coursing car Pushpaka and it knew his mind and came to him straightaway. He searched the west and north and east and south."

Can we say, "No, these things are not true?" when all of mythology and legend speak either directly of or in parallel to these things? And even in the Holy Bible may be found strange references:

"In the same hour came forth fingers of a man's hand, and wrote over against the candlestick upon the plaster of the wall of the King's palace; and the King saw that part that he wrote."

Daniel 5:5

This we do know from observations made via the Portals that LeMuria and Atlantis did exist and they did attain to great cultures and high civilizations before sinking beneath the ocean. Also at one time a continent existed south of India, between India and the northwestern coast of Australia. On this land was established the first colony from the Antarctic Continent civilization.

It was by the use of these Portals that part of the exploration of the great tunnel system that networks the entire globe was accomplished, including the vast yards full of trains and the main station terminal below Rainbow City. By the use of these Portals the many "sealing off" doors to the tunnels were found and opened, in preparation for train passage through on the lines we desired to operate.

It is quite evident that these Portals are operating under reduced power at present but our group expects to have them running at full strength soon. Then further exploration of space may be possible as well as increased penetration in other lines of research.

Consider how handy these Portals are for the research scientists who, upon discovering an ancient ruin or anything else of the past, may at will - almost with the speed of thought - examine its history from beginning to end.

The Tunnels

The great underground city beneath the surface at Rainbow City is built and strengthened by an odd metal, the same as used in the construction of the railroad tunnels and terminals. This metal is made by a machine that takes the raw earth and rock and turns it, by some atomic manipulation, into a soft, plastic-like metal that slowly hardens. When this metal has finally set to its full hardness, an atomic cutting torch takes five hours to cut one and one half inches.

This underground city was used for manufacturing, food processing, and artificial growing, as well as storage space and living quarters for workers. It surrounds the great tunnel depot terminal and its vast yards are stored with great trains ready for use. Elevators and ramps are commonly used to all sections and levels. Light is furnished by some sort of "cold light" process which gives off beneficial rays of the sun. The air in the city as well as the tunnels seems to be revitalized from or by these same lamp sources.

At the fifth lower level of the underground city is the main depot and traffic office and dispatcher system that controls the entire network of train tunnels throughout the world. There is also a communication system for voice and vision to all trains and to all terminals and their branch lines. The tunnels of the main lines are always dual, one above the other, and operate on a one-way system of handling trains.

The tunnels are lined with the tough metal which supports and reinforces the underground city. Each tunnel has a diameter somewhat over one hundred feet. The trains arc about one hundred feet in diameter and each coach length is three and one half times its diameter, each engine two times its diameter.

When in operation the trains float free of all walls; when at rest they fit into grooved channels in the side walls.

Fastest Trains In The World

The top speed of these trains is unknown to us at present, but our group of scientists tested them well above two thousand miles per hour. As to air resistance and pressure within the tunnels at this speed we do not at present know the answer, they are made of tough metal, the same as used is the tunnel linings.

At present only a few mainlines and their terminals and trunk lines and branches have been used by our associate's party. But according to the tunnel map routes these tunnels run deep underground and spread throughout the entire world, beneath the seas and land surfaces in all directions. Of the tunnels explored, one branch line ends in what is now a swamp in the heart of South America. Here, from the evidence of old ruins in the vicinity, was once a great sea port and thriving city of ancient times on an ancient seashore. According to the Maps of today, this is in the upper reaches of the present Amazon river in that mysterious district in which a number of explorers from the United States and other countries have gene into and from which they have not returned.

Another tunnel ends in a new-closed cave in the southwestern part of the United States in an Indian territory or reservation. Another branch line ends in northwestern Wyoming, due west of Sheridan and some two hundred feet or more up the side of a mountain. This tunnel seems to have been twisted and sheared off, leaving a distorted and pinched outlet. When we consider the great density and toughness of the metal lining the tunnels, a metal that even earthquakes and great land mass movements cannot break, we wonder what titanic force sheared and twisted the Sheridan tunnel end. When we have time we shall use the Portals to find the answer.

At tunnel ends and all terminals there are great doors that seal each tunnel, section by section, and all tunnels are empty. Only the terminal depots have any machinery in them, and these are for handling freight and fighting equipment.

Each terminal depot is a great storehouse of numerous levels deep for medical supplies, concentrated foods and food essences, and concentrates of what today might be called vitamins, a tablespoon measure of which will relieve all fatigue and need of nourishment, liquid or sleep for over twenty-four hours with modern man today. Here too are stored many fighting machines and quantities of small arms (personal equipment) for army uses. These are mostly atomic blaster types.

All of this perhaps stored over one or two million years ago, yet still in perfect condition.

The Egyptian Book of the Dead Again

These terminals may be the far famed and often written of "Tunnels of the Earth" perhaps referred to in the Egyptian Book of the Dead:

"I am the offspring of yesterday; the tunnels of the earth have given me birth; and I am revealed at my appointed time."

Also:

"It is I who carry away thy might, that I may come and seize upon the tunnels of Ra."

Chapter 108.

All tunnels are lighted by a cold light system similar to that in the great underground city and the air vitalized in the same manner, terminals likewise. According to the comparisons of modern maps with the ancient ones, the tunnels are in a vast network underlying just about all nation today, and reaching many regions that today are inaccessible to modern man, referred to only in mythology, such as the sunken continent of Atlantis and the lost LeMuria of the Pacific ocean.

By the evidence of the Portals and the ancient maps, great civilizations did exist and an interchange of commerce linked them together through their common heritage with the Motherland, at the present south Polar continent. Star maps of the ancient days established a fair estimate of the time when all of this was in use.

Entrances Covered

Most tunnel openings have long since been covered by land slides and shifts in earth structures and only a few at this time remain open to the outside world, some in Tibet, Siberia and Africa, as well as South America and North America. There are some entrances in the interior of certain remote islands.

One train alone can carry enough troops and their equipment, modern style, to completely make up a small army. These trains are five-decked inside and have a tremendous capacity of load and storage. Automatic equipment for safety, capable of handling emergency and normal usage at the tremendous speeds involved, is built into all trains and terminals. As we have said before these trains float free from all contacts with the walls by some means that we have not solved yet.

The trains are entirely sealed when in operation and carry their own atmosphere.

The cold-light used in the trains evidently revitalizes and conditions the air in the trains in the same manner as is done in the underground city.

Access To Secret Treasure Via Tunnel

By Portal examination we have found that the Inca's fabled hoard of wealth was concealed in a tunnel mouth-end in the Andes mountains. It still remains there, untouched by our party.

Why?.

Just consider yourself living in the midst of untold wealth (according to present worldly standards) with all wants of material necessities and substance at hand for use, of living amongst luxury as is not yet known in modern times, of being a part of this Eden, where the monetary unit called by us money, can buy nothing. This is a place where one finds a peace of mind and soul beyond and above the hurry-scurry of this, our present day so-called civilization.

To give one an idea of the size of the tunnel train terminals which handled local traffic out into the system, and from which many single branch lines stem from or pass through, the average length and width is about four miles. The depth from top to bottom is about three hundred feet. There are over ten levels for storage and for offices.

In these terminals were found three-wheeled vehicles for loading and unloading as well as passenger carrying, and ramps to accommodate them. Elevators reached all levels. There were official's offices with Portal machines as part of the equipment, file and record rooms to handle all the detailed traffic of commerce that at sometime must have moved through them. There were tremendous rooms for clerks and all of their necessary equipment and dispatcher's rooms with tremendous control boards to allow contact with the trails as well as other terminals.

The elevators made contact with the tops of these terminals which, by the evidence found at one time, were on the surface of the earth, Some now are buried deep by the shifting of land masses, In some localities on this earth it was found that these terminal top entrances were close to the earth's surface, and not many hundreds of feet of excavation of debris would be needed to free the entrances for usage.

It is here that a very strong question arises in our minds as well as yours: Why such an elaborate transportation system, so well designed and built to last for ages, should be in evidence; unless we should come to this conclusion, that at one time in the earth's (pre) historic past a very great and expanded civilization must have been spread all over the then earth's surface, possibly by colonization from the Motherland at the Antarctic continent, or possibly by a great mass transplanting of the human species from the planet now known to us as Mars.

Only time will tell the answers and believe us truly when we say that there seem to be millions of questions that need asking and solving.

Analysis of the Dole Flight to Hawaii Portal

In the long ago history of mankind, during the time of the civilization of LeMuria, its scientists developed great machines to act as transmitters and receivers of metals and certain organic substances. These machines were used to transport these material substances between earth and the moon. Living organic matter was carried by Space Ships traversing the space between earth and moon.

Air is still to be found in the deep caverns of the moon and life still exists there . But the human race has long since degenerated from its original status to a condition beyond belief due to the fact that contact with the earth was broken off 21,000 years ago when LeMuria sank beneath the waves of the Pacific ocean. The descendants of humanity of the moon who lived and worked there traveled between moon and earth. Their mythology is colorfully alive with reference to fire spitting and fire breathing dragons... (Space Ships)

We have previously stated and we insist that mythology is but a garbled, distorted and mistranslated history of the ancient Mankind. Research will unfold a valuable addition to the understanding of today's human races; and as we remove the veil of mystery step by step, will reveal their common kinship and brotherhood.

We moderns have for too long smugly considered ourselves as superior in achievement and learning, and think that mythology is a mixture of superstitious belief and vague mysteries, to be interpreted in some far off manner as a thing apart from our everyday life. Yet we constantly cry to the very heavens for help to be rescued from the chaos of our own thoughts and acts. Mythology is a long pattern of humanity's achievements and mistakes, and the glory achieved by humanity when they follow the right path. It also gives the penalties for disobeying God's laws.

The great machine transmitters and receivers that once linked the moon-peoples with earth have long ago stopped working, with the exception of one transmitter on earth and one partially operative receiver on the moon.

The transmitter still working here on earth is situated on a submerged part of LeMuria; now the floor of the Pacific ocean on a line midway between San Francisco and the Hawaiian Islands, perhaps a little-north. This location we cannot at the present time positively identify, but it is this area that both surface vessels and airships avoid. How big it is we do not know, though it seems to quite large in area. Vessels entering its sphere of influence disappear and are never heard from again.

It was here that the historical "Dole Flight" was lost in 1927. The San Francisco "Examiner's" plane carried a radio signal generator powered by an air-driven generator which made known the speed of the plane. That and the radio operator's remarks before going into the silence are ample proof of something strange in this area, but it is no longer mysterious. That was history and may be found in detail in the back files of the San Francisco newspapers, especially the Examiner.

The transmitting machine seemed to push, and at the same time disintegrate, any metal or organic substance above it, toward the moon. The receiver functioned as a collector of the beam and re-assembled into its original form the material sent.

They operated automatically.

On the moon near the partially functioning receiver are scattered bits of wreckage, amongst which are bits of planes, all that is left of the Dole flight.

The bodies of the humans are lost in space, possibly in an orbit circling the stars.

INNER EARTH AND HOLLOW EARTH MYSTERIES
RICHARD SHAVER'S DERO - NAZI AND ALIEN UNDERGROUND BASES

WHAT IS THE SHAVER MYSTERY?

Here Is A Mystery That Stretches From The Madhouse To The White House — From Superstition To Scientific Knowledge - From the Forgotten Past To The Present! There are those who support Richard Shaver in his honey-comb of caverns the world over populated by a demented race know as the Dero, the greatest evil the earth has ever know. This is his story in his own words (and others who have undergone the same hell).

JUST RELEASED: ( ) The Hidden World NO. 7 This Issue Contains Two Shocking Stories by RIchard S. Shaver: **FORMULA FROM THE UNDERGROUND - THE WOMB OF TITAN, and THE RED LEGION - STRUGGLE OF NATIVE AMERICANS IN THE CAVERNS** Plus JOURNEY THROUGH THE CAVES - HOME OF THE TEN LOST TRIBES OF ISRAEL

( ) NUMBER 6 - Entering The Secret Vaults Of The Elders - The Hollow World And The Ten Lost Tribes - Readers Reaction To Voices From The Caves.

( ) NUMBER 5—Deeds of the Elder Race? - Exploring The Occult Underground - The True Sorceress: Ladies of the Cavern World - Inner Earth: Fact? Fiction? Theory? Science?

( ) NUMBER 4—Reality of the Sathanas, Forbidden Playground of the Underworld. - The Madness of Richard Shaver.

( ) NUMBER 3—Mantong: The story of the Messiah as told in the caves. Underground rail system to hell. Death Rays from the Inner Earth.

( ) NUMBER 2—Airplane crashes, train wrecks, celebrity deaths caused by demented Dero. The dark cloud expands over Earth as subsurface mutants kidnap, torture and eat humans.

( ) NUMBER 1—Tormenting voices from the cavens. The home of ancients below Earth. Mantong, an unknown language.

Additional Volumes Will Be Added. . . Each volume approx 200 pages. Large format. $25.00 each. Any 4 books $$88.00. **All 7 just $159.95.** Add sufficient postage and handling (see our rate chart on order form).

Global Communications • Box 753 • New Brunswick, NJ 08903

( ) Best of Hollow Earth Hassle — There are two sets of unorthodox beliefs about the interior of our planet – the theory that the earth may be hollow and possibly inhabited (by a race of giants?) and that a system of caverns exists beneath our feet that are controlled by both good and evil entities (thus the concept of a hell below). Features a series of shocking articles from rare newsletter of same name. $21.95
ISBN: 978-1606110195 - Large Edition - Illustrated

( ) The Cave Of The Ancients —T. Lobsang Rampa enters the subterranean abode to meet with the Masters in the Halls of The Akashic Records. Deep inside Earth, it is revealed to the honorable monk fascinating accounts of ancient space visitors, lost civilizations, advanced gravity ships, and much more knowledge long forgotten by humankind. — $21.95
ISBN: 978-1606110607 - Large Edition

( ) Inner Earth And Outer Space People - Rev. Wm Blessing examines the inner earth from a Biblical viewpoint. CENSORED FOR CENTURIES BY THE CHURCH WITH THE BACKING OF WORLD LEADERS! Is There A Golden Paradise Inside Our Earth? Who Pilots The Ships We Call UFOs? Are They Here To Harm Or Help Us? Are The Residents Of This Subterranean World Angels or Devils? - $29.95
ISBN: 978-1606110362 -Large Edition - 320 pages - Illustrated

( ) Mysteries of Mount Shasta: Home Of The Underground Dwellers and Ancient Gods — SACRED SITE? ENTRANCE TO THE INNER EARTH? HIDDEN UFO BASE? TIME WARP? BLACK HOLE? Come with journalist Tim Beckley as he explores the US's most mysterious place. Lemurians and survivors of other "Lost Civilizations" roam the mountain, occasionally wandering into town to trade gold for supplies. Native Americans residing here say they have not only heard the screams of Bigfoot, but have seen these hairy creatures close-up! Visit Telos, the capitol of the Inner Earth occupied by the Ascended Masters of Wisdom — $21.95 —ISBN: 978-1606110027 - Large Edition - Illustrated

( ) Etidorhpa - Strange History of a Mysterious Being and an Account of a Remarkable Journey — A member of a secret society, John Uri Lord travels with a "sightless," superhuman to a subterranean land of magic and wonderment most will never see. Distant Worlds. Dead Civilizations. Other Dimensions. Rare reprint - $24.95
ISBN: 978-1892062185 - Large Edition - Illustrated

( ) Finding Lost Atlantis Inside The Hollow Earth - Brinsley Le Poer Trench (a member of the House of Lords) takes the reader on an exploration like no other. Here are tales of polar openings, hidden civilizations, strange underground races, Admiral Byrd's Top Secret discoveries, the central sun, the Shaver Mystery and much more that will open your eyes to a new reality like never before! Underground, the Atlantians still live in peace and tranquility away from the war-like elements upon the surface. — $21.95
ISBN: 978-1892062819 - Illustrated

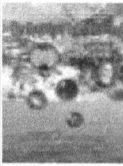

( ) The Mysterious Cyrus Teed: The Phenomenon Of The Hollow Earth —. While working in his lab and hoping to find the Philosopher's Stone and convert lead into gold, Teed saw a beautiful woman who revealed that he was to become a messiah and reveal the true cosmogony to the world. It was at this point that his particular hollow earth theory began to take shape. - $21.95
ISBN 978-1606110713 - Nearly 300 pages - Illustrated

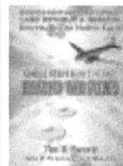

( ) Admiral Richard E. Byrd's Journey Beyond The Poles — Tim Swartz examines the great explorer's journey to the mythological lands of Hyperborea and Ultima Thule. His meeting with strange beings at the poles. His discovery of a secret Nazi base there. The development of German Flying Saucers. Britian's Secret War with Hitler's henchmen. Most important story of all time being hidden under our very noses. - $19.95
( ) Add $15.00 for ADMIRAL BYRD'S MISSING DIARY!
ISBN: 978-0938294986 - Large Edition - Documents -